MODEL AND ALGORITHMS FOR SCHEDULING UNIFORM PARALLEL MACHINES

P SENTHILKUMAR

AMAZON

Model and Algorithms for Scheduling Uniform Parallel Machines
P. Senthilkumar

ISBN: 9798876627759

Published by Amazon Self-Publishing Kindle Edition (Paperback)

Published by Dr.P.Senthilkumar
Address: No.20, Second Cross Street, Kalaivani Nagar, Pethichettipet, Lawspet, Pondicherry-605 008

DEDICATION

The author dedicates this text to all his teachers

TABLE OF CONTENTS

PREFACE

Production scheduling helps businesses become more productive and efficiently satisfy consumer needs. Because it falls within the combinatorial category, scheduling work on uniform parallel computers to minimize the makespan measure is a difficult problem under single machine scheduling. The goal of this essay is to show how to design an effective algorithm for this particular situation.

The introduction chapter of this text covers single machine scheduling with a single machine, single machine scheduling with parallel machines, and research gap of unform parallel machine scheduling.

The goals of the challenge, the assumptions behind the scheduling of uniform parallel machines, and the plan for developing the algorithms are all presented in Chapter 2, which describes the problem. A model and an example of the model utilizing a small size problem are provided in Chapter 3 on the mathematical model for uniform parallel machines scheduling to minimize makespan. The simulated annealing algorithm to minimize makespan in the single machine scheduling problem with uniform parallel machines is presented in Chapter 4. It includes an overview of the algorithm, its skeleton, three newly developed simulated annealing algorithms, and a comparison of them to determine which is the best.

The development of a GA-based strategy to reduce the uniform parallel machine scheduling makespan is presented in Chapter 5. This covers the basic structure of the genetic algorithm, factors that impact the GA algorithm, techniques for assigning tasks to machines, and crossover strategies. Additionally, it entails the creation of four GA-based heuristics to reduce makespan and a comparison of them to determine which GA-based heuristic is optimum for scheduling jobs on uniform parallel computers.

In order to determine which is optimal, the best GA-based heuristic and the best simulated annealing technique are compared in Chapter 6 to minimize the makespan of scheduling jobs on uniform parallel computers. Appendix 1 for replication 1 and Appendix 2 for replication 2 contain the data needed to test the heuristics in Chapter 4, Chapter 5, and Chapter 6.

The author expresses gratitude to all of his university colleagues and academicians for their support in releasing this work. The writing style of this text is simple to read.

P. Senthilkumar, B.E., M.E., Ph.D

1 INTRODUCTION

1. 1 INTRODUCTION

Production scheduling, which attempts to create a schedule for producing a variety of products in accordance with the company's production strategy, is a crucial task in every business. Consequently, this enhances the production of the organization. The following are the categories under which production scheduling falls.

1. Scheduling using a single machine only

2. Scheduling problem for a single machine with multiple parallel machines

3. Scheduling for flow shops

4. Schedules for job shops

5. Scheduling for open shops

6. Scheduling in batches

1.2 SINGLE MACHINE SCHEDULING WITH SINGLE MACHINE

There will be n jobs with a single operation that must be completed on a single machine in single machine scheduling. The following is a list of the features of the single machine scheduling problem.

- It has n jobs that each have a single operation and sequence-independent processing times. As a result, each job's processing time includes its preparation time.
- It just has one machine, which is always on call and never left idle when work is being done.
- Each job's processing time (t_j) is known ahead of time (t_j, j = 1, 2, 3,..., n).

- Every job's ready time (rj) is taken to be zero (rj = 0, j = 1, 2, 3,... n)
- A job is processed continuously until it is finished, no matter what happens, which indicates that it is not allowed to preempt jobs.

The following is a set of performance metrics for the single machine scheduling problem with n independent jobs.

- Reducing the average flow time
- Reducing total tardiness
- Reducing the number of jobs that are late.
- Reducing the maximum amount of tardiness.

The average of the work completion times is known as the mean flow time. The shortest processing time rule, or SPT rule, can be used to optimize this measure. In order to reduce the mean flow time, the jobs must be placed in increasing order of processing times.

Reducing the overall tardiness is a crucial metric, which translates to reducing the average tardiness.

Let n be the number of jobs that each involve a single operation.
Let Cj represent the job j's completion time.
Let dj represent the job j's due date.
Tj is the job j's tardiness.

$$\text{Tardiness, } T_j = \text{Max}[\ 0,\ C_j - d_j\ ], \text{ if } C_j > d_j$$
$$= 0, \text{ otherwise}$$

$$\text{Total tardiness } = \sum_{j=1}^{n} T_j$$

The best answer for this performance metric can be found using a branch and bound algorithm or a mathematical model. Because branch and bound methods and mathematical models are very difficult to apply when solving large-scale problems, practitioners employ heuristics to find near-optimal solutions for these kinds of problems fast. An objective-focused rule of thumb is called a heuristic. This refers to a clearly laid out process that relies on intuition to find the optimal answer to the issue at hand.

The maximum lateness values of the jobs are the definition of maximum lateness. If a task takes longer to complete than the scheduled delivery date, its lateness is determined by subtracting the completion time from the promised delivery date. This performance measure is minimized by applying the EDD (Earliest Due Date) rule. This rule states that in order to reduce the maximum amount of lateness, the jobs must be ordered in increasing order of their due dates.

Reducing the number of late jobs is an additional metric for evaluating success in the single machine scheduling issue. This refers to the quantity of late work. If a task is finished after the deadline, it is considered late.

1.3 SINGLE MACHINE SCHEDULING WITH PARALLEL MACHINES

If there are several machines in the single machine scheduling problem, it is referred to as a single machine scheduling problem with parallel machines. A novel performance metric called makespan is thought to be significant in this kind of issue. Each parallel machine will have the completion time of the final job scheduled on it when m parallel machines are used to schedule n independent jobs, each involving a single operation. The maximum of these completion times across all machines is the makespan of the parallel machines scheduling problem. Reducing the makespan is the primary objective of researchers in this kind of problem.

Identical and non-identical parallel machines can be used to categories the parallel machines scheduling problem. Uniform parallel machines and unrelated parallel machines are two further classifications for the non-identical parallel machines.

These are mentioned in the list below.

1. The scheduling problem for identical parallel machines

2. Scheduling problem for uniform parallel machines

3. A scheduling problem with unrelated parallel machines.

Let tij represent the task j's processing time on machine i for i = 1, 2, 3,... m and j = 1, 2, 3,... n.

This processing time is then used to specify the aforementioned problems.

i.   The problem is referred to as an identical parallel machine scheduling problem if tij = t1j for all i and j.

      This indicates that the speeds of each parallel machine are the same. Every single work on every single parallel machine will process in the same amount of time.

ii.   The problem is referred to be a uniform (proportional) parallel machines scheduling problem if tij = t1j/si for all i and j, where si is the machine i's speed and t1j is the task j's processing time on machine 1. The parallel machines' speeds will be in increasing order in this kind of problem.

      This implies that the speeds of the parallel machines will differ. For the parallel machines 1, 2, 3,... and m, respectively, we often assume s1, s2, s3,... and sm with the relation s1 < s2 < s3 <.. < sm. In other words, machine m is the quickest machine, and machine 1 is the slowest. The processing times for a particular job on the parallel machines will fall into the following ratio.

$$1/s_1 : 1/s_2 : 1/s_3 : \ .... : 1/s_m.$$

iii.   The problem is referred to as an unrelated parallel machine scheduling problem if tij is arbitrary for all i and j.

The processing times of a job on the parallel machines will not be related in this kind of scheduling. This could be the result of various employment characteristics, machine technological variations, etc.

1.3.1 Identical Parallel Machines Scheduling

The characteristics of the identical parallel machines scheduling problem with the objective of minimizing makespan are as listed below.

- It has n jobs that each have a single operation and sequence-independent processing times. As a result, each job's processing time includes its preparation time.
- It has m identically paced parallel machines. ($s_1 = s_2 = s_3 = ... = s_m$)
- Machines are never idle while a task is pending; they are always available.
- The jobs' processing timed (tj, j = 1, 2, 3,..., n) are known ahead of time.
- It is assumed that each job has a zero ready time (rj = 0, j = 1, 2, 3,... n).

The following is a list of properties of the identical parallel machines scheduling problem where the goal is to minimize makespan.

- It has n jobs that each have a single operation and sequence-independent processing times. As a result, each job's processing time includes its preparation time.
- It has m identically paced parallel machines. (sm = s1 + s2 + s3 =...)
- Machines are never idle while a task is pending; they are always available.
- The jobs' processing timeframes (tj, j = 1, 2, 3,..., n) are known ahead of time.
- A job is processed continuously until it is finished, no matter what happens. This indicates that it is not allowed to preempt jobs.

An example is provided to illustrate the idea of makespan on the identical parallel computers. Examine the processing durations of six jobs, which need to be scheduled as indicated in Table 1.1 on two parallel machines.

Table 1.1 Processing Times of Jobs on Identical Parallel Machines

	Processing time t_j (minutes)					
Job j	1	2	3	4	5	6
Processing time t_j	10	8	5	12	4	6

Th Gantt chart of assigning the jobs of the sequence 1-2-3-4-5-6 to two parallel machine is shown Fig.1.1.

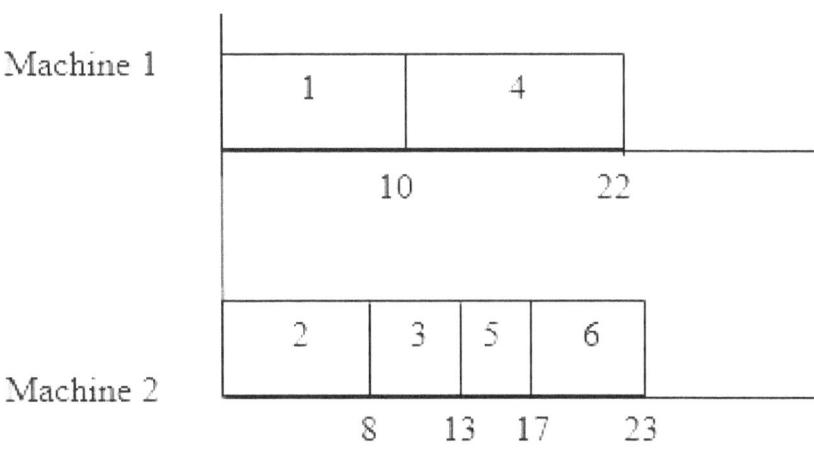

Fig.1.1 Gantt Chart of Identical Parallel Machines Scheduling

It is evident from Fig. 1.1 that the schedule's makespan is 23 minutes. The makespan of the relevant schedule will differ from that of the order of assignment 1-2-3-4-5-6 if we assign the jobs to the parallel machines assuming a different sequence of jobs, such as 6-5-4-3-2-1. This demonstrates unequivocally that the makespan is determined by the order in which the jobs are assigned to the machines.

1.3.2 Uniform Parallel Machines Scheduling

The characteristics of the uniform parallel machines scheduling problem with the objective of minimizing makespan are as listed below.

The following is a summary of the features of the uniform parallel machines scheduling problem when the goal is to minimize makespan.

- Its n single operation jobs have sequence-independent processing times. As a result, each job's processing time includes its preparation time.
- It contains m parallel machines that operate at various speeds (s1 < s2 < s3 <.. < sm).

5

- Machines are never idle while a task is pending; they are always available.
- The jobs' processing times (tij, i = 1, 2, 3,... and j = 1, 2, 3,... n) are known ahead of time.
- The processing times of each work on the uniform parallel machines are inversely related to their respective speeds (1/s1: 1/s2: 1/s3:.. : 1/sm).
- It is assumed that each job has a zero ready time (rj = 0, j = 1, 2, 3,... n).
- A job is processed continuously until it is finished, no matter what happens. This indicates that it is not allowed to preempt jobs.

The goal of this study is to minimize the time it takes to schedule n independent jobs that each require a single operation on m uniform parallel machines. Table 1.2 displays the data for a sample single machine scheduling problem with uniform parallel machines that has two machines and six jobs. It is evident from this table that the speeds of machine 1 and machine 2 are, respectively, 1 and 2.

Table 1.2 Processing Times of Jobs on Uniform Parallel Machines

Machine i	Speed Ratio	Job j					
		1	2	3	4	5	6
1	1	10	8	5	12	4	6
2	2	5	4	2.5	6	2	3

The Gantt chart of scheduling the jobs as per the sequence 1-2-3-4-5-6 on two parallel machines is shown in Fig.1.2.

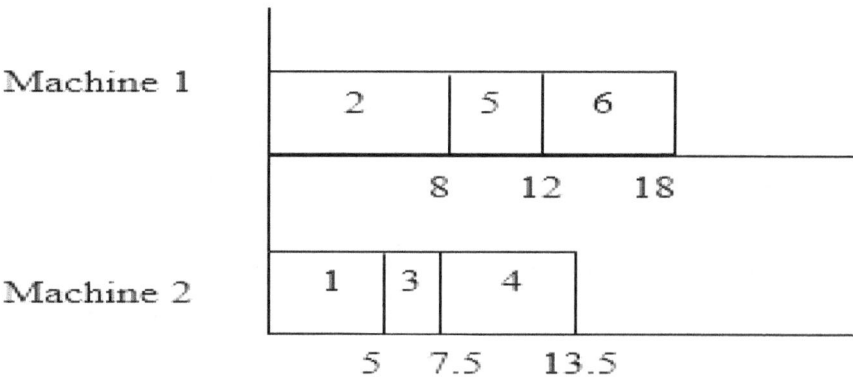

Fig.1.2 Gantt Chart of Uniform Parallel Machines Scheduling

The last work on machine 1 took 18 minutes to complete, while the last job on machine 2 took 13.5 minutes to complete, according to Figure 1.2. The makespan of the schedule, as illustrated in Fig. 1.2, is 18 minutes, the maximum of these two variables. When assigning the jobs to uniform parallel machines, if we assume a different sequence of jobs, such as 6-5-4-3-2-1, the makespan of the associated schedule will differ from the results we obtained for the order of assignment of the jobs, 1-2-3-4-5-6. This demonstrates unequivocally that the makespan is determined by the sequence in which the jobs are assigned to the uniform parallel machines.

1.3   RESEARCH GAP

Through literature, it has been found that there is a need to develop an efficient heuristic to schedule jobs on uniform parallel to machines to minimize their makespan. The rest of the chapters are devoted in this direction.

REVIEW QUESTIONS

1. Classify production scheduling problem.
2. Talk about the single machine scheduling problem's underlying presumptions.
3. Enumerate and describe the performance metrics for the scheduling problem involving a single machine.
4. Describe and enumerate the types of single machine scheduling using parallel machines.
5. Explain the scheduling problem with identical parallel machines.
6. Describe the scheduling problem for uniform parallel machines.
7. Provide an example of how jobs are scheduled on uniform parallel machines

2. PROBLEM DESCRIPTION

2.1 INTRODUCTION

This chapter presents the research's assumptions, objectives, and explanation of the problem.

Uniform parallel machines, identical parallel machines, and unrelated parallel machines are the three categories of single machine scheduling difficulties involving parallel machines that were previously discussed. This includes the scheduling problem for a single machine with parallel machines. This text considers the single machine scheduling problem with uniform parallel machines. While many performance metrics are taken into account in this research, the scheduling of n independent single operation jobs on m uniform parallel machines of the single machine scheduling problem is the main emphasis, since makespan minimization is an integrated measure.

2.2 ASSUMPTIONS OF UNIFORM PARALLEL MACHINES

The following is a summary of the features of the uniform parallel machines scheduling problem when the objective of minimizing minimize makespan, as already stated in Chapter 1.

- Its n single operation jobs have sequence-independent processing times. As a result, each job's processing time includes its preparation time.
- It contains m parallel machines that operate at various speeds ($s_1 < s_2 < s_3 < .. < s_m$).
- Machines are never idle while a task is pending; they are always available.
- The jobs' processing times (t_{ij}, $i = 1, 2, 3,...$ and $j = 1, 2, 3,... n$) are known ahead of time.
- The processing times of each work on the uniform parallel machines are inversely related to their respective speeds ($1/s_1: 1/s_2: 1/s_3:.. : 1/s_m$).

- It is assumed that each job has a zero ready time (rj = 0, j = 1, 2, 3,... n).
- A job is processed continuously until it is finished, no matter what happens. This indicates that it is not allowed to preempt jobs.

2.3 OBJECTIVES OF THE RESEARCH

There are numerous performance metrics for the uniform parallel machine single machine scheduling problem. The makespan minimization is taken into consideration in this study. Table 2.1 displays a generalized format of the job processing times in the single machine scheduling problem with uniform parallel machines.

Table 2.1 Generalized Format of Processing Times of Jobs

		Job j						
		1	2	3	.	j	.	n
Machine i	1	t_{11}	t_{12}	t_{13}	.	t_{1j}	.	t_{1n}
	2	t_{21}	t_{22}	t_{23}	.	t_{2j}	.	t_{2n}
	3	t_{31}	t_{32}	t_{33}	.	t_{3j}	.	t_{3n}
	.	.	.	.	.	.	.	.
	i	t_{i1}	t_{i2}	t_{i3}	.	t_{ij}	.	t_{in}
	.	.	.	.	.	.	.	.
	m	t_{m1}	t_{m2}	t_{m3}	.	t_{mj}	.	t_{mn}

Let, n be the number of independent jobs

t_{ij} is the processing time of the job j on the machine i,

for i = 1, 2, 3, .., m and j = 1, 2, 3, ..., n.

Further, $t_{ij} = t_{1j}/s_i$ for all i = 2, 3, ..., m and j = 1, 2, 3, ..., n.
C_i be the completion time of the last job on the machine i

Let, n be the number of jobs. For each of the values of i varies from 1 to m and j varies from to n, tij represents the processing time of job j on machine i. Moreover, for all i = 2, 3,.. m and j = 1, 2, 3,.. n, tij = t1j/si. Let C_i be the moment at which the last task on the machine is finished.

Makespan (M) =   Maximum { C_i }

i = 1,2,3, ..m

This means that the makespan of scheduling the given n independent single operation jobs on m uniform parallel machines is the maximum of the completion times of the last jobs in all the machines.

A sample problem with 6 independent single operation jobs and 2 uniform parallel machines is already shown in the Table 1.2 of the section 1.3.2 which is reproduced in Table 2.2. Let us consider the jobs as per the order 1-2-3-4-5-6, one by one and assign them to the two uniform parallel machines as shown in Fig.2.1, for which the makespan is 18.

This indicates that the maximum of the final task completion durations across all machines is the makespan of scheduling the specified n independent single operation jobs on m uniform parallel machines.

A sample problem with two uniform parallel machines and six distinct single operation jobs is shown in Table 2.2. The jobs in the order 1-2-3-4-5-6 will be examined one at a time, and they will be assigned to the two uniform parallel machines as seen in Fig. 2.1, for which the makespan is 18.

Table 2.2 Processing Times of Jobs on Uniform Parallel Machines

Machine i	Speed Ratio	Job j					
		1	2	3	4	5	6
1	1	10	8	5	12	4	6
2	2	5	4	2.5	6	2	3

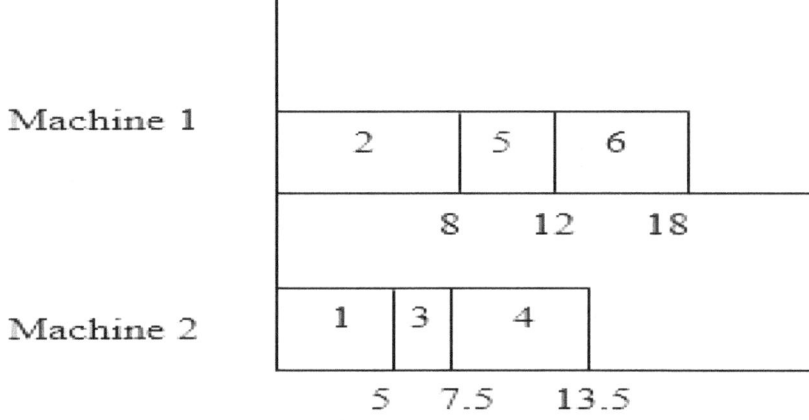

Fig.2.1 Gantt Chart of Uniform Parallel Machines Scheduling

It is evident from Fig. 2.1 that the maximum of the last job completion durations across all machines is the makespan of scheduling the specified n independent single operation jobs on m parallel machines.

2.4   PLAN OF ALGORITHMS DEVELOPMENTS
The following is a plan of development for a meta-heuristic to minimize the makespan of the uniform parallel machines single machine scheduling problem.
    1. A review of the research problem's literature
    2. The creation of an algorithm for simulated annealing
        2.1 Creation of a set of simulated annealing algorithms to reduce the makespan of a uniform parallel machine single machine scheduling problem.

2.2 A comparison of how well the various simulated annealing techniques performed in terms of choosing the optimal simulated annealing algorithm and minimizing the makespan of the single machine scheduling problem with homogeneous parallel machine

3. The creation of a heuristic based on GA

3.1 Creation of four GA-based heuristics based on various crossover techniques and machine task distribution strategies during initial population generation.

3.2 Evaluate the various GA-based heuristics and choose the best one.

4. This study aims to compare the best simulated annealing algorithm and the best GA-based heuristic for minimizing the makespan of the single machine scheduling problem with uniform parallel machines. The recommendation is to select the best algorithm between the two to determine the minimum makespan of the problem.

REVIEW QUESTIONS

1. State the assumptions of uniform parallel machines.
2. What are the objectives of the development of algorithms to minimize the makespan of uniform parallel machine scheduling.

3 MATHEMATICAL MODEL FOR UNIFORM PARALLEL MACHINES SCHEDULING TO MINIMIZE MAKESPAN

3.1 INTRODUCTION

An optimal solution to a problem can be found using a mathematical model. Whenever a combinatorial problem arises, a metaheuristic must be developed. This calls for a comparison between the meta heuristic's solution and the best one. As a result, for a particular problem, the deviation between the metaheuristic and mathematical model solutions can be found by comparing the numerical model and model solutions. Thus, a makespan minimization mathematical model for the uniform parallel machine scheduling problem is introduced.

3.2 MATHEMATICAL MODEL

A mathematical model can be used to determine the best makespan for scheduling n independent single operation jobs on m uniform parallel computers. For this problem, a mathematical model is provided.

The count of the single operation jobs, which are independent is n

The count of the parallel machines is m

t_{ij} is the time of processing of the job j on the machine i for i = 1, 2, 3, ..., m and j = 1, 2, 3, ..., n &

$t_{ij} = t_{1j}/s_i$ for all i = 2, 3, ..., *m* and j = 1, 2, 3, ..., *n*.

The formula for the makespan, *M* is as given below.

A mathematical model can be used to determine the best makespan for scheduling n independent single operation jobs on m uniform parallel machines. For this problem, a mathematical model is provided.

Let n be the total number of separate tasks involving a single operation and m be the number of machines operating in parallel.

let tij be the processing time of the job j on the machine i. for all i and j

tij = t1j/si for all i = 2, 3,.., m and j = 1, 2, 3,.., n,

The following is the formula for the makespan, or M.

$$M = Max \sum_{j=1}^{n} t_{ij}X_{ij}, i = 1, 2, 3, \dots, m \qquad \dots\dots\dots 3.1$$

where, X_{ij} = 1, if the job j is assigned to the machine i
= 0, otherwise
for i = 1, 2, 3, ..., m and j = 1, 2, 3, ..., n.

A descriptive mathematical model to minimize the makespan of the problem is shown below.

Minimize Z= $Max \sum_{j=1}^{n} t_{ij}X_{ij}, i = 1, 2, 3, \dots, m$

Subject to

$$\sum_{i=1}^{m} X_{ij} = 1, j = 1, 2, 3, \dots, n \dots\dots\dots 3.3 \ ..$$

where, X_{ij} = 1, if the job j is assigned to the machine i
= 0, otherwise,   for i = 1, 2, 3, ..., m and j = 1, 2, 3, ..., n

In this particular model, there are mn variables and n total constraints. The objective function in this model is in descriptive form, making it unsolvable. To remedy the issue, a different version of this model is therefore required.

Thus, the makespan of scheduling n independent single operation jobs on m uniform parallel computers can be found using the linear mathematical model that is shown below.

Minimize Z1 = M 3.4

Subject to

$$M - \sum_{j=1}^{n} t_{ij}X_{ij} \geq 0, \ i = 1, 2, 3, \dots, m \qquad \dots\dots\dots 3.5$$

$$\sum_{i=1}^{m} X_{ij} = 1, j = 1, 2, 3, \dots, n \dots\dots\dots \qquad \dots\dots\dots 3.6$$

where, X_{ij} = 1, if the job j is assigned to the machine i
= 0, otherwise,   for i = 1, 2, 3, ..., m and j = 1, 2, 3, ..., n
$M \geq 0$ and it is the makespan of the schedule.

In this particular model, there are mn+1 variables and m+n total constraints. This problem falls into the domain of combinatorics.

3.3 MODEL ILLUSTRATION OF MODEL

In this part, the model for the single machine scheduling problem with uniform parallel machines is applied to a situation involving four uniform machines and nine jobs. The machines' speed ratio is 1:2:3:4. The problem's data are displayed in Table 3.3.

Table 3.3 Processing Times of Jobs of 4 Machines and 9 Jobs Problem

(Uniform parallel Machines)

Problem Size	Machine	Job Number								
		1	2	3	4	5	6	7	8	9
4X9	1	36	144	178	188	67	188	85	18	42
	2	18	72	89	94	33	94	42	9	21
	3	12	48	59	62	22	62	28	6	14
	4	9	36	44	47	16	47	21	4	10

The following is a mathematical model for this problem. There is one non-negative variable and thirty-six zero-one type variables in this model. There are thirteen constraints in this model.

<u>Mathematical Model</u>
Minimize $Z = M$

Subject to
$M - 36x_{11} - 144x_{12} - 178x_{13} - 188x_{14} - 67x_{15} - 188x_{16} - 85x_{17} - 18x_{18} - 42x_{19} \geq 0$
$M - 18x_{21} - 72x_{22} - 89x_{23} - 94x_{24} - 33x_{25} - 94x_{26} - 42x_{27} - 9x_{28} - 21x_{29} \geq 0$
$M - 12x_{31} - 48x_{32} - 59x_{33} - 62x_{34} - 22x_{35} - 62x_{36} - 28x_{37} - 6x_{38} - 14x_{39} \geq 0$
$M - 9x_{41} - 36x_{42} - 44x_{43} - 47x_{44} - 16x_{45} - 47x_{46} - 21x_{47} - 4x_{48} - 10x_{49} \geq 0$

$\quad\quad x_{11} + x_{21} + x_{31} + x_{41} = 1$
$\quad\quad x_{12} + x_{22} + x_{32} + x_{42} = 1$
$\quad\quad x_{13} + x_{23} + x_{33} + x_{43} = 1$
$\quad\quad x_{14} + x_{24} + x_{34} + x_{44} = 1$
$\quad\quad x_{15} + x_{25} + x_{35} + x_{45} = 1$
$\quad\quad x_{16} + x_{26} + x_{36} + x_{46} = 1$
$\quad\quad x_{17} + x_{27} + x_{37} + x_{47} = 1$
$\quad\quad x_{18} + x_{28} + x_{38} + x_{48} = 1$
$\quad\quad x_{19} + x_{29} + x_{39} + x_{49} = 1$

$x_{ij} = 0$ or 1, for $i = 1, 2, 3, 4$ & $j = 1, 2, 3, 4, 5, 6, 7, 8, 9$ and $M \geq 0$
The results of this model are presented below.

$\quad\quad\quad x_{17} = 1$
$\quad\quad\quad x_{24} = 1$
$\quad\quad\quad x_{31} = 1$
$\quad\quad\quad x_{35} = 1$
$\quad\quad\quad x_{36} = 1$
$\quad\quad\quad x_{42} = 1$
$\quad\quad\quad x_{43} = 1$
$\quad\quad\quad x_{48} = 1$

$$x_{49} = 1$$
Makespan (M) = 96 minutes

The assignments of the jobs to different machines are shown in Table 3.4 and the corresponding Gantt chart is shown in Fig.3.2.

Table 3.4 Assignments of Jobs to Machines

Machine	Assigned jobs
1	7
2	4
3	1, 5, 6
4	2, 3, 8, 9

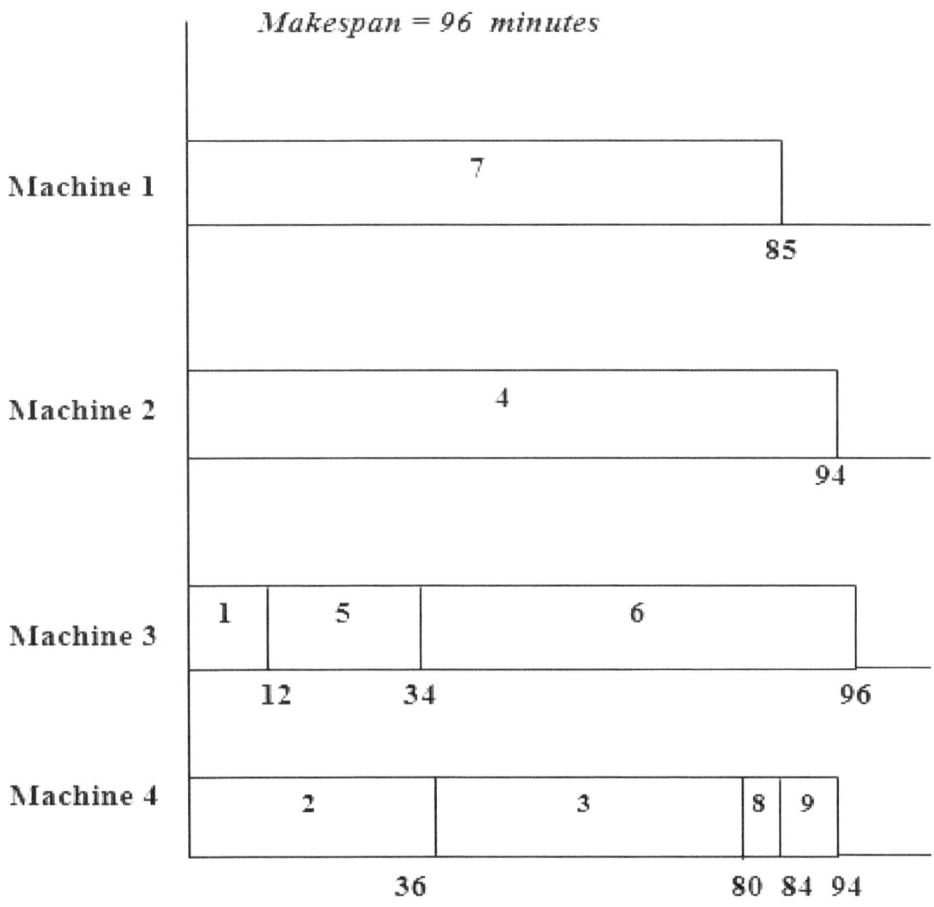

Fig.3.2 Gantt chart of the problem 4X9 using mathematical model

Both the number of variables and restrictions will be high for problems of a significant magnitude. The number of variables and model constraints that any software used to tackle this kind of problem can handle is limited. Therefore, using heuristics to find close to optimal solutions is inevitable. The most accurate solution will be provided by meta-heuristics. Therefore, an attempt has been made in this study to create two distinct meta-heuristics and compare them to recommend the most effective one for use.

REVIEW QUESTIONS

1. Give the necessity for mathematical model to solve combinatorial problem.
2. Give the mathematical model to minimize the makespan of scheduling jobs on uniform parallel machines.
3. Illustrate the development of mathematical model to minimize the makespan of scheduling jobs on uniform parallel machines.

4.SIMULATED ANNEALING ALGORITHM FOR SINGLE MACHINE SCHEDULING PROBLEM WITH UNIFORM PARALLEL MACHINES TO MINIMIZE MAKESPAN

4.1 INTRODUCTION TO SIMULATED ANNEALING ALGORITHM

In order to minimize the makespan in the single machine scheduling problem with uniform parallel machines, this chapter provides a simulated annealing approach. The heat treatment method of annealing gave rise to the simulated annealing algorithm. The goal of annealing is to restore the metallurgical structure of cold-drawn, hammered, and other components. By releasing the internal stress and strain of the component, a heat treatment procedure known as "annealing" will restore the misaligned grain structure to its natural state. The annealing process described above, known as the "simulated annealing algorithm," is utilized to solve optimization problems, particularly combinatorial ones. The following are the parameters of the simulated annealing algorithm:

T – a temperature to be set for the experiment

r – a reduction factor from 0 to 1 to reduce the temperature

δ – a small positive constant

The macro steps of the simulated annealing algorithm for minimization problem are presented below.

Step 0: Enter r, δ, and T.

Step 1: Obtain a preliminary workable solution S_o and calculate the objective function f(So)'s corresponding value.

Step 2: Assume the starting temperature (T > 0).

Step 3: In the vicinity of So, generate a workable solution S1, and determine the associated value of the objective function f(S1).

Step 4: Determine d = f(S0) - f(S1).

Step 5: Update S_o.

Step 5.1: Proceed to Step 6 after setting S_o = S_1 if d > 0; if not, proceed to

Step 5.2.

Step 5.2: Create a uniformly distributed random number between 0 and 1 (R) in step 5.2.

Step 5.3: Set So = S1 and proceed to Step 6 if R < $e^{(d/T)}$; if not, proceed to Step 6.

Step 6: Update $T = r \times T$

Step 7: Check whether $T > \delta$.

If yes, go to *Step 3*; otherwise go to *Step 8*.

Step 8: Now starting from the last S_o, use local optimization to reach a local optimum solution.

Step 9: Stop

The following list identifies the three perturbation strategies used in simulated annealing.

i)   Transferring a task from one machine to another.

ii)   Switching jobs between two machines.

iii)   Moving a job from an existing machine to a new machine (this kind of scheduling makes this approach unworkable).

In the third plan, the job that is transferred from any of the current machines will require the inclusion of a new machine. There is a set number of machines (m) in the given problem. Therefore, it is not possible to use the third scheme of perturbation.

The simulated annealing algorithm's skeleton makes it evident that, to find a decent solution, researchers need first employ an effective seed generation approach, which should be followed by the second phase to find the global optimal solution.

4.2 SEED GENERATION ALGORITHM

This section presents the steps of a seed generation technique used in the simulated annealing algorithm. The initial assignment of jobs to the machines and the exchange/transfer of work among machines comprise Parts 1 and 2 of this seed generation method.

Part 1 Allocation of Jobs to the Machines

Step 1: Enter the data below.

• The numbery (n) of jobs involving a single operation

• The number (m) of identical parallel machines with velocities s1, s2, s3,... sm.

• The jobs' processing times on the uniform parallel machines.

• The previous maximum makespan (PMS) (10^6 very high)

Step 2: Rearrange the jobs in the machine 1 processing order (decreasing order of processing time from left to right) according to their longest processing times.

Step 3: Execute the following, going left to right, for each task Q (that is, Q = 1, 2, 3,... n) in the longest processing time order array.

   3.1 Add the present job to each machine as the last job, and calculate the job's temporary completion time for each machine.

   3.2 Determine the machine number (P) that corresponds to the minimum (MIN) of the job's temporary completion times on each machine.

   3.3: Make the following updates:

      a) The final job on the machine P was completed in MIN.

      b) Increase the number of jobs assigned to machine P by 1.
$N(P) = N(P) + 1$

      c) As indicated below, store the current job Q on machine P at position N(P).
$JOB_{P, N(P)} = Q$

Step 4: Determine the maximum time of the completion times of the last jobs on all machines and use that as the makespan (MS) of the current schedule.

   Assume that R is the machine where this maximum makespan happens.

Part 2 Exchange/ Transfer of Jobs among the Machines

Step 5: Check whether MS ≥ PM.

   If so, proceed to Step 8; if not, modify PMS = MS and proceed to Step 6.

If they yield reduction in makespan. Interchanging the jobs between machines starting from machine R to Machine 1

Step 6: Initialize INDEX1 = 0

Step 7: Execute the following for each task (job at position I) on the machine R, going from left to right: I = 1, 2, 3,... N(R).

   7.1 Initialize I = 1

   7.2 Find the machine X other than the machine R, on which the job at the position I on the machine R takes least time.

   7.3 Compute completion time of the last job on the machine X after temporarily transferring the job on the position I on the machine R to the position after the current last job on the machine X.
   Let the last job completion time on machine X be CT_X.

   7.4 Locate the machine Y, excluding machine R, where the last job's completion time is the shortest.

   7.5 Compute the last job on the machine Y after temporarily transferring the job at the position I on the machine R to the position after the current last job on the machine Y.
   Let it be CT_Y.

   7.6 Find the minimum of CT_X and CT_Y. Lit it be MCT and the respective machine be Z.

   7.7 Check whether MCT is greater than or equal to MS.

If yes, Go to Step 7.10; else go to Step 7.8.

7.8 Update the following.

MS = MCT and the corresponding solution after effecting the transfer of the job at the position I on the machine R to the position after the last job on the machine Z.

7.9 Check whether MS is greater than or equal to PMS.

If yes, go to Step 7.10; else update the following.

PMS = MS

Best schedule of the jobs

INDEX =1

7.10 Increase the job position on the machine R by 1 (I = I + 1)

7.11 Check whether I is less than or equal to the number of jobs on the machine R.

If yes, go to Step 7.2; else go to Step 7.12.

7.12 Check whether INDEX is 1.

If yes, go to Step 5; else go to Step 8.

Step 8: Print the best result and the respective makespan PMS.

Step 9: Stop.

4.3 SIMULATED ANNEALING ALGORITHM TO MINIMIZE MAKESPAN

This section presents three distinct simulated annealing strategies (SA1, SA2, and SA3) designed to minimize the makespan in the uniform parallel machine single machine scheduling problem. The methods used by these algorithms to choose the machines for job exchanges and job transfers between machines differ from one another. Table 4.1 presents the details.

Table 4.1 Distinctions Among the SA Algorithms Applied to Minimize Makespan

Algorithm	Probability of selection of machines for exchanging jobs	Probability of selection of machines for transferring a job from one machine to another machine
SA_1	Proportional to the speed indices of the machines	Proportional to the speed indices of the machines
SA_2	Proportional to the reverse of the speed indices of the machines	Proportional to the speed indices of the machines
SA_3	Proportional to the reverse of the speed indices of the machines	Proportional to the reverse of the speed indices of the machines

The machines' speed indices are the basis for the classification in Table 4.1. Take a look at Table 4.2's sample data on the machine speed indices for an problem involving ten machines.

Table 4.2 Sample Data on Speed Indices of 10 Machine

Machine	Speed Index
1	1
2	2
3	3
4	4
5	5
6	6
7	7
8	8
9	9
10	10

The total of 10 values from 1 [m(m+1)/2, where m is the number of machines] equals 55, the sum of the speed indices.

Table 4.3 displays the probability of each machine being selected in relation to its speed index. Table 4.4 displays the probability of each machine being selected in relation to its matching speed index in reverse order.

Table 4.3 Probability of Selection of Machines Proportional to Their Corresponding Speed Indices

Machine	Speed Index	Probability of Selection of Machine
1	1	1/55
2	2	2/55
3	3	3/55
4	4	4/55
5	5	5/55
6	6	6/55
7	7	7/55
8	8	8/55
9	9	9/55
10	10	10/55

Table 4.4 Probability of Selection of Machines Proportional to Their
Corresponding Speed Indices in Reverse Order

Machine	Speed Index	Probability of Selection of Machine
1	1	10/55
2	2	9/55
3	3	8/55
4	4	7/55
5	5	6/55
6	6	5/55
7	7	4/55
8	8	3/55
9	9	2/55
10	10	1/55

Through experimentation, the parameters of the simulated annealing algorithm are set as shown below.

Temperature, $T = 60$
Reduction factor for temperature, $r = 0.85$
Control Parameter (Stopping Condition), $\delta = 0.01$.

4.3.1 Simulated Annealing Algorithm SA₁

The steps of the simulated annealing algorithm SA1 are shown in this section. With this method, two machines are chosen to swap jobs and move a job from one machine to another based on the probabilities corresponding to their speed indices, as shown in Table 4.3.

Step 1: Take the following as input.
- Count of single operation jobs, which are independent, n
- Count of uniform parallel machines (m) with speeds $s_1, s_2, s_3, ...,$ s_m.
- Times of processing times of the jobs on the uniform parallel machines.

Step 2: Using the seed generation algorithm given in Section 4.2, find the initial feasible solution (S_0). The corresponding solution in terms of makespan is $f(S_0)$.

Step 3: Initialize $T = 60$, $r = 0.85$ and $\delta = 0.01$.

Step 4: In the neighborhood of S_0, obtain a feasible solution S_1 and let its makespan be $f(S_1)$.

Step 4.1: Generate random number in between 0 and 0.99, which is uniformly distributed.

Step 4.2: Check whether R is less than or equal to 0.49.

If yes, go to *Step* 4.3; else go to *Step* 4.4.

Step 4.3: Macro step of Exchanging of jobs between two machines.

  Step 4.3.1: Based on the probability which is proportional to the speed as shown in the Table 4.3, select a machine (P1) which has a minimum of one job.

  Step 4.3.2: On the machine P1, select a job randomly and assume the selected job as Q1.

  Step 4.3.3: Based on the probability which is proportional to the speed as shown in the Table 4.3, select another machine (P2) which has a minimum of one job.

  Step 4.3.4: On the machine P2, select a job randomly and assume the selected job as Q2.

  Step 4.3.5: Swap the jobs Q1 and Q2 among the machines P1 and P2.

  Step 4.3.6: Calculate $f(S_1)$, which is the makespan of this schedule and then go to *Step* 5.

Step 4.4: *Macro step of transferring a job from one machine to another machine.*

  Step 4.4.1: Based on the probability which is proportional to the speed as shown in the Table 4.3, select a machine (P1) which has a minimum of one job.

  Step 4.4.2: On the machine P1, select a job randomly and assume the selected job as Q1.

  Step 4.4.3: Based on the probability which is proportional to the speed as shown in the Table 4.3, select another machine (P2), which will receive the job Q1.

  Step 4.4.4: Now, move the job Q1 to the machine P2.

  Step 4.4.5: Calculate $f(S_1)$, which is the makespan of this schedule and then go to *Step* 5.

Step 5: Determine the difference between the solution of the initial solution and the current solution: $d = f(S_0) - f(S_1)$.

Step 6: *Steps of updating S_o based on the value of d.*

  Step 6.1: Check whether *d* is more than 0.

    If yes, store S_1 in S_o and then go to Step 7; else go to Step 6.2.

  Step 6.2: Obtain a random number (R) in the range from 0 to 0.99, which is uniformly distributed

  Step 6.3: Check whether *R* is less than $e^{(d/T)}$.

    If yes, store S_1 in S_o and then go to Step 7; else go to Step 7.

Step 7: Reduce the temperature *T* using the following formula.

  $T = r \times T$

Step 8: Check whether *T* is more than δ.

If yes, go to *Step 4*; else go to *Step* 9.

Step 9: Reach a local optimum beginning at the last S_0 value by utilizing the second part of the seed generation process (local optimum method from Step 5 to Step 12) and print the final schedule.

Step 10: Stop.

4.3.2 Simulated Annealing Algorithm SA₂

This section presents the steps of the simulated annealing algorithm, SA2. Using this approach, two machines are chosen for a job exchange, and each machine is chosen with a probability proportionate to its matching speed in reverse order. In the process of moving a job from one machine to another, each machine is chosen with a probability that varies according to its speed.

Step 1: Input the following.
- Count of single operation jobs, which are independent, n
- Count of uniform parallel machines (*m*) with speeds s_1, s_2, s_3, ..., s_m.
- Times of processing of the jobs on the uniform parallel machines.

Step 2: Using the seed generation algorithm given in Section 4.2, find the initial feasible solution (S_0). The corresponding solution in terms of makespan is $f(S_0)$.

Step 3: Initialize $T = 60$, $r = 0.85$ and $\delta = 0.01$.

Step 4: In the neighborhood of S_0, obtain a feasible solution S_1 and let its makespan be $f(S_1)$.

    Step 4.1: Generate random number in between 0 and 0.99, which is uniformly distributed.

    Step 4.2: Check whether R is less than or equal to 0.49.
        If yes, go to *Step* 4.3; else go to *Step* 4.4.

    Step 4.3: Macro step of Exchanging of jobs between two machines

        Step 4.3.1: Based on the probability which is proportional to the speed in reverse order as shown in the Table 4.4, select a machine (P1) which has a minimum of one job.

        Step 4.3.2: On the machine P1, select a job randomly and assume the selected job as Q1.

        Step 4.3.3: Based on the probability which is proportional to the speed in reverse order as shown in the Table 4.4, select another machine (P2) which has a minimum of one job.

        Step 4.3.4: On the machine P2, select a job randomly and assume the selected job as Q2.

        Step 4.3.5: Swap the jobs Q1 and Q2 among the machines P1 and P2.

        Step 4.3.6: Calculate $f(S_1)$, which is the makespan of this schedule and then go to *Step* 5.

Step 4.4: *Macro step of transferring a job from one machine to another machine.*

> *Step* 4.4.1: Based on the probability which is proportional to the speed as shown in the Table 4.3, select a machine (P1) which has a minimum of one job.
>
> *Step* 4.4.2: On the machine P1, select a job randomly and assume the selected job as Q1.
>
> *Step* 4.4.3: Based on the probability which is proportional to the speed as shown in the Table 4.3, select another machine (P2), which will receive the job Q1.
>
> *Step* 4.4.4: Now, move the job Q1 to the machine P2.
>
> *Step* 4.4.5: Calculate $f(S_1)$, which is the makespan of this schedule and then go to *Step* 5.

Step 5: Determine the difference between the solution of the initial solution and the current solution: $d = f(S_0) - f(S_1)$.

Step 6: *Steps of updating S_0 based on the value of d.*

> *Step* 6.1: Check whether d is more than 0.
>
> > If yes, store S_1 in S_0 and then go to Step 7; else go to Step 6.2.
>
> *Step* 6.2: Obtain a random number (R) in the range from 0 to 0.99, which is uniformly distributed
>
> *Step* 6.3: Check whether R is less than $e^{(d/T)}$.
>
> > If yes, store S_1 in S_0 and then go to Step 7; else go to Step 7.

Step 7: Reduce the temperature T using the following formula.

$$T = r \times T$$

Step 8: Check whether T is more than δ.

> If yes, go to *Step* 4; else go to *Step* 9.

Step 9: Reach a local optimum beginning at the last S_0 value by utilizing the second part of the seed generation process (local optimum method from Step 5 to Step 12) and print the final schedule.

Step 10: Stop.

4.3.3 Simulated Annealing Algorithm SA3

This section presents the steps of the simulated annealing algorithm SA3. This method selects two machines with a probability proportional to their respective speeds in reverse order, in order to exchange jobs and move jobs from one machine to another.

Step 1: Input the following.

- Count of single operation independent jobs, n
- Count of uniform parallel machines (m) with speeds s_1, s_2, s_3, ..., s_m.
- Times of processing of the jobs on the uniform parallel machines.

Step 2: Using the seed generation algorithm given in Section 4.2, find the initial feasible solution (S_0). The corresponding solution in terms of makespan is $f(S_0)$.

Step 3: Initialize $T = 60$, $r = 0.85$ and $\delta = 0.01$.

Step 4: In the neighborhood of S_0, obtain a feasible solution S_1 and let its makespan be $f(S_1)$.

    Step 4.1: Generate random number in between 0 and 0.99, which is uniformly distributed.

    Step 4.2: Check whether R is less than or equal to 0.49.
        If yes, go to *Step* 4.3; else go to *Step* 4.4.

    Step 4.3: Macro step of Exchanging of jobs between two machines.

        Step 4.3.1: Based on the probability which is proportional to the speed in reverse order as in Table 4.4, select a machine (P1) which has a minimum of one job.

        Step 4.3.2: On the machine P1, select a job randomly and assume the selected job as Q1.

        Step 4.3.3: Based on the probability which is proportional to the speed in reverse order, select another machine (P2) which has a minimum of one job.

        Step 4.3.4: On the machine P2, select a job randomly and assume the selected job as Q2.

        Step 4.3.5: Swap the jobs Q1 and Q2 among the machines P1 and P2.

        Step 4.3.6: Calculate $f(S_1)$, which is the makespan of this schedule and then go to *Step* 5.

    Step 4.4: *Macro step of transferring a job from one machine to another machine.*

        Step 4.4.1: Based on the probability which is proportional to the speed in reverse order as in Table 4.4, select a machine (P1) which has a minimum of one job.

        Step 4.4.2: On the machine P1, select a job randomly and assume the selected job as Q1.

        Step 4.4.3: Based on the probability which is proportional to the speed in reverse order as in Table 4.4, select another machine (P2), which will receive the job Q1.

        Step 4.4.4: Now, move the job Q1 to the machine P2.

        Step 4.4.5: Calculate $f(S_1)$, which is the makespan of this schedule and then go to *Step* 5.

Step 5: Determine the difference between the solution of the initial solution and the current solution: $d = f(S_0) - f(S_1)$.

Step 6: *Steps of updating S_0 based on the value of d.*

Step 6.1: Check whether *d* is more than 0.

  If yes, store S_1 in S_o and then go to Step 7; else go to Step 6.2.

Step 6.2: Obtain a random number (R) in the range from 0 to 0.99, which is uniformly distributed

Step 6.3: Check whether *R* is less than $e^{(d/T)}$.

  If yes, store S_1 in S_o and then go to Step 7; else go to Step 7.

Step 7: Reduce the temperature *T* using the following formula.

  $T = r \times T$

Step 8: Check whether *T* is more than δ.

  If yes, go to *Step 4*; else go to *Step* 9.

Step 9: Reach a local optimum beginning at the last S_o value by utilizing the second part of the seed generation process (local optimum method from Step 5 to Step 12) and print the final schedule.

Step 10: Stop.

4.4 EXPERIMENTATION WITH THE ALGORITHMS

As previously mentioned, three simulated annealing techniques are provided in this chapter. Comparing them in terms of their solutions is the next stage, therefore. To compare the three simulated annealing techniques, a complete factorial experiment with two replications is used in the experiment design. The number of jobs in this experiment ranges from 11 to 25, while the number of machines varies from 2 to 10.

Data on processing times have been randomly generated by assuming the speed indices equal to the corresponding job indices (Speed Index 1 for Machine 1, Speed Index 2 for Machine 2,..., Speed Index m for Machine m) for each combination of the number of uniform parallel machines and the number of jobs which are to be scheduled in them. Appendix 1 contains the data. Appendix 1 displays the replication 1 data according to the factorial experiment in its entirety, while Appendix 2 displays the replication 2 data according to the factorial experiment in its entirety. For every experimental combination, the makespan values of the problems are obtained. The Table 4.5 displays the outcomes of the makespan values.

An ANOVA with three components is used to analyze the makespan values in Table 4.5. The model for this analysis is shown below.

The whole factorial experiment model, which was utilized to examine the information in Table 4.2, is displayed below.

$Y_{ijk} = \mu + P_i + A_j + PA_{ij} + e_{ijk}$,

where

- o Y_{ijk} represents the makespan of the kth replication in relation to the jth algorithm treatment (Factor B) and the ith problem size (Factor A).
- o Let μ be the total mean.

- o The impact of Factor A's treatment on the makespan is represented by the letter A_i.
- o The impact of Factor B's j^{th} treatment on the makespan is denoted by B_j.
- o The impact of Factor A's i^{th} treatment and Factor B's j^{th} treatment on the makespan is represented by AB_{ij}.
- o With respect to the ith treatment of the problem size (Factor A) and the jth treatment of the algorithm (Factor B),
- o e_{ijk} is the random error linked to the makespan of the kth replication.

The experiment's hypotheses are listed below.

Factor A: Problem Size

H0: In terms of makespan, there are no appreciable differences between the problems.

H1: For at least one pair of problems, there is a notable difference in the makespan between the problems.

Factor B (Algorithm)

H0: The makespan of the three algorithms (SA1, SA2, and SA3) is not significantly different from one another.

H1: For at least one pair of algorithms, there is a notable difference in the makespan between the algorithms (SA1, SA2, and SA3).

Factor AB (Problem Size X Algorithm)

H0: In terms of the makespan, there is no significant difference between the interaction terms of Factor A and Factor B.

H1: In terms of makespan, there is a considerable variation between the interaction terms of Factor A and Factor B.

Table 4.6 presents a summary of the ANOVA results.

Table 4.5 Results of SA Algorithms

Problem Size	Makespan		
	SA_1	SA_2	SA_3
2X11	203.0	199.0	203.5
	183.0	179.0	177.0
2X12	204.5	201.5	202.0
	200.0	193.0	200.0
2X13	255.0	256.0	255.5
	206.0	205.0	204.0
2X14	222.0	225.0	225.0
	275.0	280.0	275.0
2X15	338.5	338.0	338.5
	263.0	264.0	264.0
2X16	286.0	287.0	285.5
	286.0	284.0	284.0
2X17	330.0	333.0	332.5
	322.0	323.0	326.0
2X18	376.5	376.5	375.0
	277.0	277.0	277.0
2X19	320.0	320.5	321.5
	358.0	358.0	356.0
2X20	299.0	300.0	299.0
	445.0	445.0	443.0
2X21	407.0	407.0	407.0
	310.0	312.0	310.0
2X22	408.5	408.0	409.0
	410.0	409.0	413.0
2X23	401.0	399.5	400.5
	391.0	391.0	391.0
2X24	361.0	361.0	361.0
	414.0	415.0	415.0
2X25	465.0	466.5	465.0
	499.0	499.0	500.0

Table 4.5 Results of SA Algorithms

Problem Size	Makespan		
	SA_1	SA_2	SA_3
3X11	86.0	86.0	85.3
	86.0	86.0	86.0
3X12	122.0	122.0	122.0
	120.0	120.0	118.0
3X13	124.0	127.0	119.0
	110.0	110.0	104.0
3X14	122.5	121.5	122.5
	131.0	131.0	131.0
3X15	141.0	144.0	146.0
	129.0	126.0	127.0
3X16	152.3	150.0	152.3
	164.0	165.0	165.0
3X17	168.5	168.5	168.5
	137.0	138.0	138.0
3X18	152.0	152.0	149.5
	162.0	164.0	163.0
3X19	197.0	199.0	198.7
	192.0	187.0	192.0
3X20	188.5	189.0	189.0
	190.0	189.0	189.0
3X21	210.5	214.0	211.5
	198.0	200.0	200.0
3X22	214.3	218.0	218.0
	195.0	195.0	195.0
3X23	224.0	221.0	223.0
	212.0	210.0	212.0
3X24	215.0	215.0	215.0
	205.0	205.0	205.0
3X25	208.0	206.0	212.0
	242.0	237.0	240.0

Table 4.5 Results of SA Algorithms

Problem Size	Makespan		
	SA_1	SA_2	SA_3
4X11	58.0	59.3	59.3
	61.0	61.0	60.0
4X12	78.0	78.0	75.3
	64.0	64.0	63.0
4X13	69.0	69.0	69.0
	80.0	81.0	80.0
4X14	75.0	76.8	76.8
	76.0	76.0	76.0
4X15	86.7	86.7	86.8
	84.0	84.0	84.0
4X16	82.3	84.3	84.3
	98.0	99.0	97.0
4X17	93.0	93.0	90.0
	93.0	93.0	93.0
4X18	111.0	111.0	109.0
	95.0	95.0	91.0
4X19	107.0	107.0	107.0
	104.0	104.0	104.0
4X20	105.5	105.5	105.5
	115.0	115.0	115.0
4X21	124.0	127.5	127.5
	134.0	135.0	136.0
4X22	121.7	121.7	118.5
	133.0	133.0	133.0
4X23	133.3	131.8	135.0
	140.0	140.0	139.0
4X24	143.0	140.0	142.0
	116.0	119.0	119.0
4X25	145.7	149.3	149.3
	147.0	147.0	147.0

Table 4.5 Results of SA Algorithms

Problem Size	Makespan		
	SA$_1$	SA$_2$	SA$_3$
5X11	46.0	44.4	46.0
	51.0	51.0	51.0
5X12	51.5	51.5	51.5
	46.0	46.0	46.0
5X13	57.0	57.0	57.0
	43.0	43.0	43.0
5X14	52.0	52.0	52.0
	49.0	48.0	49.0
5X15	53.4	53.4	52.0
	56.0	56.0	56.0
5X16	68.5	68.5	68.5
	52.0	57.0	57.0
5X17	68.0	68.0	68.0
	64.0	64.0	64.0
5X18	67.4	67.4	67.3
	71.0	71.0	71.0
5X19	65.5	65.5	65.5
	91.0	91.0	91.0
5X20	69.0	67.8	69.0
	54.0	57.0	55.0
5X21	87.5	87.5	87.5
	91.0	91.0	91.0
5X22	88.0	88.0	88.0
	85.0	82.0	85.0
5X23	87.0	87.0	86.8
	86.0	85.0	81.0
5X24	86.3	87.4	87.4
	103.0	103.0	103.0
5X25	92.5	92.5	92.5
	94.0	94.0	94.0

Table 4.5 Results of SA Algorithms

Problem Size	Makespan		
	SA_1	SA_2	SA_3
6X11	32.2	32.2	32.2
	26.0	26.0	26.0
6X12	37.7	36.5	36.5
	33.0	35.0	35.0
6X13	30.0	30.0	30.0
	32.0	32.0	32.0
6X14	41.0	41.0	41.0
	36.0	36.0	36.0
6X15	45.8	45.8	45.8
	35.0	35.0	35.0
6X16	46.6	46.6	46.6
	44.0	44.0	43.0
6X17	51.3	51.3	51.3
	39.0	39.0	39.0
6X18	51.3	51.3	51.3
	48.0	48.0	48.0
6X19	45.8	45.8	45.8
	49.0	49.0	49.0
6X20	61.3	61.3	61.3
	53.0	53.0	53.0
6X21	51.5	51.5	51.5
	54.0	54.0	54.0
6X22	61.8	61.8	61.8
	55.0	55.0	55.0
6X23	62.0	62.0	62.0
	72.0	72.0	72.0
6X24	63.0	63.0	63.0
	57.0	57.0	57.0
6X25	73.7	73.7	73.7
	74.0	74.0	74.0

Table 4.5 Results of SA Algorithms

Problem Size	Makespan		
	SA$_1$	SA$_2$	SA$_3$
7X11	20.0	19.3	20.0
	27.0	27.0	27.0
7X12	24.5	25.4	25.4
	26.0	26.0	26.0
7X13	27.8	27.8	27.0
	26.0	26.0	26.0
7X14	27.9	27.9	27.9
	30.0	30.0	30.0
7X15	29.5	29.5	29.5
	29.0	29.0	29.0
7X16	37.7	37.7	37.7
	30.0	30.0	30.0
7X17	39.0	39.0	39.0
	37.0	37.0	37.0
7X18	34.0	34.0	34.0
	33.0	33.0	33.0
7X19	46.4	46.4	46.4
	45.0	45.0	42.0
7X20	42.2	42.2	42.2
	46.0	46.0	46.0
7X21	42.5	42.5	42.5
	42.0	42.0	41.0
7X22	48.3	48.3	48.3
	49.0	49.0	49.0
7X23	47.0	47.0	47.0
	51.0	51.0	51.0
7X24	51.6	51.6	51.6
	49.0	49.0	49.0
7X25	49.3	49.3	49.3
	45.0	45.0	45.0

Table 4.5 Results of SA Algorithms

Problem Size	Makespan		
	SA$_1$	SA$_2$	SA$_3$
8X11	18.3	18.3	18.3
	21.0	21.0	21.0
8X12	23.9	23.9	23.9
	21.0	21.0	21.0
8X13	21.6	21.6	21.6
	25.0	25.0	25.0
8X14	26.0	26.0	26.0
	21.0	21.0	21.0
8X15	27.0	27.0	27.0
	26.0	26.0	26.0
8X16	23.0	23.0	23.0
	26.0	26.0	26.0
8X17	30.0	30.0	30.0
	25.0	25.0	25.0
8X18	31.6	31.6	31.6
	26.0	26.0	26.0
8X19	30.0	30.0	30.0
	30.0	34.0	30.0
8X20	30.8	30.8	30.8
	34.0	32.0	34.0
8X21	30.0	30.0	30.0
	32.0	33.0	32.0
8X22	33.3	33.3	32.8
	33.0	30.0	33.0
8X23	34.8	34.8	34.8
	30.0	35.0	30.0
8X24	34.2	34.2	34.2
	35.0	35.0	35.0
8X25	45.0	45.0	45.0
	34.0	12.0	35.0

Table 4.5 Results of SA Algorithms

Problem Size	Makespan		
	SA$_1$	SA$_2$	SA$_3$
9X11	16.3	16.3	16.3
	12.0	12.0	12.0
9X12	16.3	16.3	16.3
	18.0	18.0	18.0
9X13	17.6	17.6	17.6
	19.0	19.0	19.0
9X14	17.5	17.5	17.5
	19.0	19.0	19.0
9X15	18.5	18.5	18.5
	18.0	18.0	18.0
9X16	21.3	21.3	21.3
	16.0	16.0	16.0
9X17	25.8	25.8	25.8
	24.0	24.0	24.0
9X18	27.3	27.3	27.3
	23.0	23.0	23.0
9X19	27.5	27.5	27.5
	29.0	29.0	29.0
9X20	28.3	28.3	28.3
	29.0	29.0	29.0
9X21	29.7	29.7	29.7
	28.0	28.0	28.0
9X22	33.0	33.0	33.0
	29.0	29.0	29.0
9X23	31.4	31.4	31.4
	27.0	27.0	27.0
9X24	33.9	33.9	33.9
	29.0	29.0	29.0
9X25	25.7	25.7	25.7
	29.0	29.0	29.0

Table 4.5 Results of SA Algorithms

Problem Size	Makespan		
	SA_1	SA_2	SA_3
10X11	10.6	10.6	10.6
	12.0	12.0	12.0
10X12	13.7	13.7	13.7
	13.0	13.0	13.0
10X13	15.0	15.0	15.0
	12.0	12.0	12.0
10X14	16.3	16.3	16.3
	17.0	17.0	17.0
10X15	16.0	16.0	16.0
	16.0	16.0	16.0
10X16	15.8	15.8	15.8
	17.0	17.0	17.0
10X17	19.8	19.8	19.8
	16.0	16.0	16.0
10X18	21.8	21.8	21.8
	21.0	21.0	21.0
10X19	23.4	23.4	23.4
	22.0	22.0	22.0
10X20	24.3	24.3	24.3
	21.0	22.0	22.0
10X21	26.4	26.1	26.4
	22.0	22.0	22.0
10X22	23.0	23.0	23.0
	22.0	22.0	22.0
10X23	24.2	24.2	24.2
	21.0	21.0	21.0
10X24	23.1	23.1	23.1
	23.0	23.0	23.0
10X25	27.0	27.0	27.0
	25.0	25.0	25.0

Table 4.6 Results of ANOVA

Source of Variation	Sum of squares	Degrees of freedom	Mean sum of squares	F_Calculated	F_table at $\alpha=0.05$	Inference
A (Problem Size)	7922713.0	134	59124.720	242.3220	1.00	**Reject Ho**
B (Algorithm)	24.5	2	12.250	0.0502	3.00	Accept Ho
AB	407.5	268	1.521	0.0062	1.00	Accept Ho
Error	98817.0	405	243.993			
Total	8021962.0	809				

Inference

Factor A (Problem Size): At a significance level of 0.05, the computed F ratio of the factor "Problem Size" is 242.322, greater than the table F ratio of 1. As a result, the null hypothesis about this factor is rejected. This indicates that the problem sizes varied significantly in terms of the makespan values.

Factor B(Algorithm): At a significance level of 0.05, the computed F ratio for the factor "Algorithm" is 0.0502, which is less than the F ratio of 3 in the table. The null hypothesis with regard to this factor is therefore accepted. This indicates that the makespan values of the algorithms do not significantly differ from one another.

Interaction AB: At a significance level of 0.05, the computed F ratio of the interaction terms is 0.0062, which is less than the table F ratio of 1. The null hypothesis with regard to this factor is therefore accepted. This indicates that, in terms of the makespan values, there is no discernible difference between the interaction terms of Problem Size and Algorithm.

It is demonstrated that the makespan of the simulated annealing algorithms does not significantly differ from one another. This suggests that SA1, SA2, and SA3, the three simulated annealing algorithms can all be employed. SA2's mean makespan (91.1) is the lowest of these simulated annealing procedure numbers. Therefore, the simulated annealing approach SA2 is recommended for the stated problem.

REVIEW QUESTIONS

1. What is simulated annealing?
2. Give the skeleton of the simulated annealing algorithm.
3. Give the steps of the seed generation algorithm used in the simulated annealing algorithm to minimize the makespan of scheduling jobs on uniform parallel machines.

4. Give the steps of SA1 to schedule jobs on uniform parallel machines to minimize the makespan.
5. Give the steps of SA2 to schedule jobs on uniform parallel machines to minimize the makespan.
6. Give the steps of SA3 to schedule jobs on uniform parallel machines to minimize the makespan.
7. Give a complete factorial experiment to compare the simulated annealing algorithms, viz. SA1 SA2 AND SA3.

5 DEVELOPMENT OF GA BASED HEURISTIC TO MINIMIZE MAKESPAN

5.1 INTRODUCTION

This chapter presents a GA-based heuristic for minimizing the makespan in a uniform parallel machine single machine scheduling problem. The mechanism of evaluation and selection is modelled by the genetic algorithm. It produces a population of successively different solutions until one is found that produces results that are acceptable. It is predicated on the fundamental mechanisms of natural selection and reproduction, which govern the evolution of biological organisms.

5.2 SKELETON OF GENETIC ALGORITHM

The skeleton of the genetic algorithm is given below **[20].**

Step1: Enter the maximum count (Q) of consecutive populations that you want to create. Let GC (generation count) equal 1.

Step 2: Obtain initial population with N chromosomes generated randomly. Denote this population by L.

Step 3: For each chromosome x, in the initial population, compute its fitness function value f(x).

Step4: As per the objective (minimization or maximization), sort L in an ascending or descending order, and then transfer a certain proportion (30%) of its chromosomes into a subpopulation P.

Step 5:. Perform the following after randomly selecting two chromosomes from the subpopulation P

   5.1 Carry out crossover operation.

   5.2 In each offspring carry out mutation for a mutation probability of α.

   5.3 Substitute the two offsprings generated in this step in the corresponding chromosomes of the larger population L.

Step 6: Execute Step 5 till the chromosomes in P are all considered for crossover.
Step 7: Increment the generation count by 1 (GC = GC + 1)
Step 8: Check whether GC is less than or equal to Q,
    If yes, go to Step 4; else go to Step 9.
Step 9: Determine which chromosome from L has the highest fitness function value, then report the results.
Step 10: Stop.

5.3 FACTORS AFFECTING GA ALGORITHM

The crossover method, mutation, the starting population's generation process, and the magnitude of the challenge are thought to have an impact on the genetic algorithm's performance.

The design parameters taken into account in this study for the GA-based heuristic are mentioned below.

- Factor A pertains to the problem size, wherein the levels are 2X11, 2X12, 2X13, ..., 2X25, 3X11, 3X12, 3X13, ..., 3X25, ..., 10X11, 10X12, 10X13, ..., and 10X25. The problem size, Factor A is determined by the number of machines and jobs.
- The "single point crossover method" and "two-point crossover method" form the levels of the crossover method (Factor B).
- The "Equal number of allocation of jobs to machines" and "Proportionate number of allocation of jobs to machines, which is based on the speed of the machines" form the levels of the initial population generation method (Factor C) are used.

5.3.1 Methods of Job Allocation to Machines

The techniques of assigning jobs to various machines during the creation of the initial population (Factor C) are explained in this section. These approaches include assigning equal numbers of jobs to machines and assigning proportionate numbers of jobs to machines.

5.3.1.1 Equal Number of Allocation Jobs to Machines (EAJ)

The building of a chromosome is described below for the method that gives each machine an equal number of jobs.

Let, NJ_i be the number of jobs assigned to machine i, i = 1, 2, 3, ..., m

$NJ_i = n/m$, if (n/m) is integer; for i = 1, 2, 3, ..., m.

Otherwise, $NJ_i = Int(n/m)$, for i =1 ,2, 3, ..., m-1

$$NJ_m = n - \sum_{i=1}^{m-1} NJ_i$$

where, n is the number of total number of jobs and m is the number of uniform parallel machines.

A sample chromosome is as shown by Chromosome 1 in Table 5.1 if there are nine jobs and three machines. Each machine number is randomly assigned to three jobs. In Table 5.1, Chromosome 2 represents an example chromosome if the number of jobs and machines are 10 and 3, respectively.

Table 5.1 Representation of Chromosomes Using equal Number of Jobs
　　　　　Assignment to　Machines

	Job Number									
	1	2	3	4	5	6	7	8	9	10
Chromosome 1:	3	1	3	2	1	3	2	1	2	
Chromosome 2:	2	3	2	1	3	1	3	2	3	1

Each gene position in the chromosome diagram above corresponds to a job number, and each gene represents a machine that is allocated a corresponding job. Genes are generated at random, contingent on the machines completing the number of jobs allocated to them.

Assuming the processing times listed in Table 5.2, the makespan for Chromosome 1 is displayed in Fig. 5.1.

Table 5.2 Processing Times of Jobs Shown in Chromosome 1 of Table 5.1

		Speed ratio	Job								
			1	2	3	4	5	6	7	8	9
	1	1	6	9	24	12	6	18	24	12	6
Machine	2	2	3	4.5	12	6	3	9	12	6	3
	3	3	2	3	8	4	2	6	8	4	2

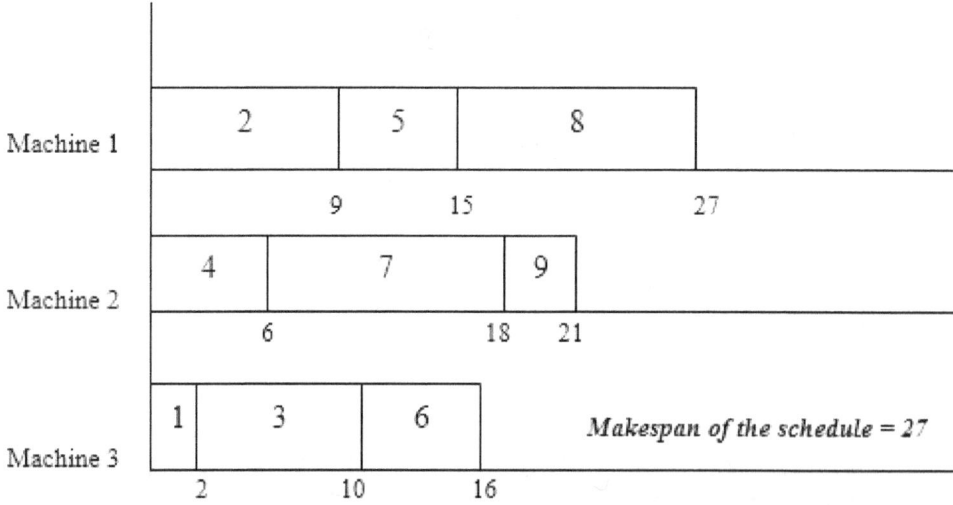

Fig.5.1 Gantt chart to determine makespan of chromosome 1 in Table 5.1

5.3.1.2 Proportionate Number of Allocation of Jobs to Machines (PAJ)

The following describes how a chromosome is constructed using the proportionate number allocation approach for machines.

Let, machines' speed ratio be $S_1: S_2 : S_3 : ....:S_m$, in which the speeds are in increasing order from machine 1

Number of jobs assigned to machine i is NJ_i, i = 1, 2, 3, ..., m

$NJ_i = Int\{[S_i/(S_1 + S_2 + S_3 + ...+ S_m)]xn\}$, if the integer value is more than 0;
    = 1, otherwise, for i = 1, 2, 3, ..., m-1

$$NJ_m = n - \sum_{i=1}^{m-1} NJ_i$$

Assume there are four machines and ten jobs. The speed ratios of the machines are one to two to three to four, correspondingly. By randomly allocating Machine 1 to one job, Machine 2 to two jobs, Machine 3 to three jobs, and Machine 4 to four jobs according to their speed ratio, Chromosome 3 in Table 5.3 presents a sample set of chromosomes for this scenario. Let us consider another scenario where there are 10 jobs and 5 machines, respectively. Assume that the machines' respective speed ratios are 1: 2: 3: 4: 5 for machines 1, 2, 3, 4, and 5, respectively.

Chromosome 4 in Table 5.3 provides an example of a chromosome for this scenario, wherein Machine 1 is assigned to one job, Machine 2 to one job, Machine 3 to two jobs, Machine 4 to two jobs, and Machine 5 to four jobs based on speed ratio.

Table 5.3 Chromosomes Representation Using Proportionate Number of Jobs Allocation to Machines

					Job Number					
	1	2	3	4	5	6	7	8	9	10
Chromosome 3:	2	1	3	4	3	4	4	2	3	4
Chromosome 4:	5	3	5	3	4	5	2	5	4	1

5.3.2 Crossover Methods

In the experiment carried out to investigate the effects of the factors on the performance of the GA-based heuristic applied to the stated problem, the single point crossover method and the two-point crossover approach are utilized in this section. These are illustrated with the chromosomes 5 and 6, which are listed below, where there are 4 machines and 10 jobs. The approach that generates these two chromosomes follows the principle of distributing jobs to machines proportionately.

```
Chromosome 5:  2   1   3   4   3   4   4   2   3   4
Chromosome 6:  4   3   4   3   2   1   2   4   3   4
```

5.3.2.1 Single Point Crossover Method

Chromosomes 5 and 6 are used to illustrate the single point crossover technique. Let 4 be the randomly chosen position among the job numbers' locations in the chromosomes, ranging from 1 to 10. Then, as can be seen below, chromosome 5 is split into two pieces, P and Q, while chromosome 6 is split into two portions, X and Y.

	P					Q				
Chromosome 5:	2	1	3	4	3	4	4	2	3	4

	X					Y				
Chromosome 6:	4	3	4	3	2	1	2	4	3	4

Below are the offspring 1 and offspring 2 that were produced by applying a single point crossover to these chromosomes.

	X					Q				
Offspring 1:	4	3	4	3	3	4	4	2	3	4

	P					Y				
Offspring 2:	2	1	3	4	2	1	2	4	3	4

5.3.2.2 Two Point Crossover Method

The same pair of chromosomes 5 and 6 is used to demonstrate the two point crossover approach. Let 3 and 6 be the two randomly chosen locations (the job numbers' locations in the chromosomes) between 1 and 10. Subsequently, as illustrated below, chromosome 5 is split into three segments, P, Q, and R, while chromosome 6 is split into three segments, X, Y, and Z.

	P			Q			R		
Chromosome 5:	2	1	3	4	3	4	4	2	3	4

	X			Y			Z		
Chromosome 6:	4	3	4	3	2	1	2	4	3	4

Below are the kids 3 and 4 that were produced by applying a two-point crossover to these chromosomes.

	X			Q			Z		
Offspring 3:	4	3	4	4	3	4	2	4	3	4

	P			Y			R		
Offspring 4:	2	1	3	3	2	1	4	2	3	4

5.4 DEVELOPMENT OF FOUR GA BASED HEURISTICS TO MINIMIZE MAKESPAN

As previously mentioned, it is primarily suspected that the following factors will have an impact on the performance of the GA-based heuristic: the "Job Allocation Method," which includes equal job allocation and proportionate job allocation, and the "Crossover Method," which includes single point and two-point crossover methods. Thus, in order to minimize the makespan, the following four (2x2=4) GA-based heuristics are presented in this part by combining the levels of these parameters.

1. GA based heuristic with single-point crossover method and equal number of jobs allocation method.

2. GA based heuristic with two-point crossover method and equal number of jobs allocation method.

3. GA based heuristic with single-point crossover method and proportionate number of jobs allocation method.

4. GA based heuristic with two-point crossover method and proportionate number of jobs allocation method.

5.4.1 GA Based Heuristic with Single-Point Crossover Method and Equal Number of Jobs Allocation Method

The following describes the steps of the GA-based heuristic that minimizes the makespan of the single machine scheduling problem with uniform parallel machines. It combines the single point crossover approach with the equal number of jobs allocation method.

Step 1: Input the following.

Number of machines (m)

Number of jobs (n) [It is assumed that n $\geq$ m]

Speed ratio of the machines: S_1: S_2 : S_3 : ....:S_m, in which $S_1 < S_2 < S_3 <$ .....: $< S_m$

Processing times $T_{i,j}$, i = 1, 2, 3, ..., m & j = 1, 2, 3, ..., n.

Mutation probability, α (0.3).

Step 2: Set the genetic algorithm parameters.

Size of population, N

Size of subpopulation, P (30% of N)

Number of iterations to be carried out, Q

Step 3: Create N chromosomes for the population by giving each machine in CHROMK, J, K = 1, 2, 3,... N and J = 1, 2, 3,.. n an equal number of jobs.

Step 4: Determine each chromosome's makespan in the population, MSK, where K = 1, 2, 3,... N.

Step 5: Initialize iteration number to 1 (q = 1).

Step 6: Arrange the chromosomes according to their makespans in ascending order. Let SCHROMK, J, K = 1, 2, 3,..., N, J = 1, 2, 3,... be the sorted chromosomes, and let MAKESPANK, K = 1, 2, 3,.., N be the array of their makespan.

Step 7: In CHROMK,J, K = 1, 2, 3, ..., N, J = 1, 2, 3, ..., n, copy the sorted chromosomes SCHROMK,J, K = 1, 2, 3, ...

Step 8: Store MAKESPAN$_1$ in BEST_MS and store SCHROM$_{1,J}$, J = 1, 2, 3, ..., n in BCHROM$_J$

Step 9: For crossover operation, the subpopulation constitutes topmost 30% of the large population .

Step 10: Initialize the count of chromosome number (C) to 1.

Step 11: After a single-point crossover of chromosomes C and C+1, the offspring C and C+1 are obtained; they are given below

Crossover between: $CHROM_{C,J}$, J = 1, 2, 3, ..., n & $CHROM_{C+1,J}$, J = 1, 2, 3, ..., n

Offspring: $OSPRING_{C,J}$, J = 1, 2, 3, ..., n & $OSPRING_{C+1,J}$, J = 1, 2, 3, ..., n

Step 12: For each offspring with a mutation probability of α, carryout mutation.

Step 13: For the offspring C and C+1, compute their makespan as MS_C and MS_{C+1}.

Step 14: Increase C by 2 (C = C + 2).

Step 15: Check whether C is less than or equal to P.

If yes, go to Step 11.

Step 16: Store the new offspring [$OSPRING_{C,J}$, C = 1, 2, 3, .., P and J =1 ,2 3, ..., n] to the chromosomes vector, $CHROM_{C,J}$, C = 1, 2, 3, ..., P and J =1, 2, 3, ., n, respectively.

Step 17: Increase q by 1.

Step 18: Check whether q is less than or equal to Q.
If yes, go to Step 6.

Step 19: Show the results as follows.
Best makespan, BEST_MS
Best chromosome, $BCHROM_J$, which is $SCHROM_{1,J}$, J = 1, 2, 3, ..., n.

Step 20: Stop

5.4.2 GA Based Heuristic with Two Point Crossover Method and Equal Number of Jobs Allocation Method

Except for Step 11, the steps are the same as those listed in Section 5.4.1. The two-point crossover's eleventh step is displayed below.

Step 11: After a two-point crossover of chromosomes C and C+1, the offspring C and C+1 are obtained. They are given below

Crossover between: $CHROM_{C,J}$, J = 1, 2, 3, ..., n & $CHROM_{C+1,J}$, J = 1, 2, 3, ..., n
Offspring: $OSPRING_{C,J}$, J = 1, 2, 3, ..., n & $OSPRING_{C+1,J}$, J = 1, 2, 3, ..., n

5.4.3 GA Based Heuristic with Single Point Crossover Method and Proportionate

Number of Jobs Allocation Method

In this algorithm only the Step 3 differs from the algorithm given in Section 5.4.1, which is given below.

Step 3: Create the population's N chromosomes by assigning the machines in each chromosome, CHROMK,J, K = 1, 2, 3,... N and J = 1, 2, 3,.. n, a proportionate number of jobs.

5.4.4 GA Based Heuristic with Two Point Crossover Method and Proportionate Number of Jobs Allocation Method

In this algorithm, the Step 3 and the Step 11 are different from those in the algorithm given in the Section 5.4.1, which are presented below.

Step 3: Create the population's N chromosomes by assigning the machines in each chromosome, CHROMK,J, K = 1, 2, 3,... N and J = 1, 2, 3,.. n, a proportionate number of jobs.

Step 11: After a two-point crossover of chromosomes C and C+1, the offspring C and C+1 are obtained. They are given below.

Crossover between: $CHROM_{C,J}$, J = 1, 2, 3, ..., n & $CHROM_{C+1,J}$, J = 1, 2, 3, ..., n

Offspring: $OSPRING_{C,J}$, J = 1, 2, 3, ..., n & $OSPRING_{C+1,J}$, J = 1, 2, 3, ..., n

5.5 COMPARISON OF GA BASED HEURISTICS TO MINIMIZE MAKESPAN

The following is a list of design criteria used in the GA-based heuristic.

- Factor A pertains to the problem size, wherein the levels are 2X11, 2X12, 2X13, ..., 2X25, 3X11, 3X12, 3X13, ..., 3X25, ..., 10X11, 10X12, 10X13, ..., and 10X25. The problem size is determined by the number of machines and jobs. Appendix 1 displays the replication 1 data according to the factorial experiment in its entirety, while Appendix 2 displays the replication 2 data according to the factorial experiment in its entirety.
- The "Single point crossover method" and "Two-point crossover method" levels are for the crossover method (Factor B).
- "Equal number of job allocation to machines" and "Proportionate number of job allocation to machines, which is based on the speed of the machines" are the levels for the method of allocating jobs to machines during the initial population generation (Factor C).

In order to minimize the makespan of the single machine scheduling problem with homogeneous parallel machines, a comparison is done between the GA based heuristics using these three parameters.

The number of jobs (n) is varied from 11 to 25 with an increment of 1, and the number of machines (m) is varied from 2 to 10 with an increment of 1. It is assumed that the machine speed ratio equals the machine number ratio. The speed ratios of machines 1, 2, 3, and 4 in a problem with four machines are 1:2:3:4, The problem sizes are 2X11, 2X12, 2X13,..., 2X25, 3X11, 3X12, 3X13,..., 3X25,..., 10X11, 10X12, 10X13,..., 10X25. There are 135 different problem sizes in total.

Two replications have been done for every combination of the factors. Thus, using the arrangement indicated in Table 5.4, 270 problems, that is, 135 problem sizes with two replications in each problem size, were generated at random. This chapter also makes use of the same data as Chapter 4.

For every experimental combination, the makespan values of the problems are obtained. Table 5.5 displays the makespan values findings. An ANOVA with three components is used to analyze the makespan values in Table 5.5. The model for this analysis is shown below.

$$Y_{ijkl} = \mu + A_i + B_j + AB_{ij} + C_k + AC_{ik} + BC_{jk} + ABC_{ijk} + e_{ijkl}$$

Where,

- The makespan value under the ith problem size, j^{th} crossover method, and k^{th} job allocation method is Y_{ijkl}.
- The makespan values' overall mean is represented by μ.
- The impact of the ith problem size on the makespan value is denoted by A_i.
- The impact of the jth crossover technique on the makespan value is denoted by B_j.
- The interaction impact between the j_{th} crossover method and the i_{th} problem size on the makespan value is denoted by AB_{ij}.
- The impact of the kth job allocation mechanism on the makespan value is denoted by C_k.
- The interaction impact between the kth job allocation technique and the ith problem size on the makespan value is known as AC_{ik}.
- The makespan value is affected by the interaction between the jth crossover technique and the kth job allocation method, which is denoted as BC_{jk}.
- The interaction impact on the makespan value of the ith problem size, j^{th} crossover method, and k^{th} job allocation method is known as ABC_{ijk}.
- With regard to the lth replication under the ith problem size, j^{th} crossover method, and k^{th} job allocation method, e_{ijkl} is the random error.

Table 5.4 Layout of Problem Generation

		Crossover Method (B)			
		Single Point		Two Point	
		Method of Allocation of Jobs (C)		Method of Allocation of Jobs (C)	
		Equal Allocation (SPCO-EAJ)	Proportionate Allocation (SPCO-PAJ)	Equal Allocation (TPCO-EAJ)	Proportionate Allocation (TPCO-PAJ)
Problem Size (A)	2X11				
	2X12				
	2X13				
	.				
	.				
	2X25				
	3X11				
	3X12				
	3X13				
	.				
	.				
	3X25				
	.				
	.				
	10X11				
	10X12				
	10X13				
	.				
	.				
	10X25				

Table 5.5 Results of GA Based Methods

Problem Size	Makespan			
	SPCO-EAJ	SPCO-PAJ	TPCO-EAJ	TPCO-PAJ
2X11	199.00	200.00	199.00	199.00
	175.00	177.00	175.00	177.00
2X12	202.50	201.50	202.50	201.50
	194.00	193.00	192.00	192.00
2X13	256.00	254.50	257.00	254.50
	201.00	202.00	201.00	202.00
2X14	221.00	220.50	221.00	220.50
	274.00	274.00	277.00	274.00
2X15	337.50	338.50	339.00	338.50
	263.00	264.00	263.00	263.00
2X16	288.00	284.50	296.50	284.00
	286.00	286.00	284.00	284.00
2X17	331.50	330.00	333.50	330.00
	331.00	322.00	324.00	322.00
2X18	377.50	375.00	375.00	374.50
	276.00	277.00	279.00	277.00
2X19	332.00	319.00	321.50	319.00
	356.00	357.00	363.00	356.00
2X20	300.00	299.00	302.00	299.00
	447.00	444.00	444.00	443.00
2X21	408.50	407.00	407.50	406.50
	312.00	310.00	322.00	310.00
2X22	408.00	407.00	407.00	407.00
	410.00	407.00	416.00	407.00
2X23	402.00	399.00	403.00	399.00
	395.00	391.00	399.00	391.00
2X24	369.00	361.00	366.00	362.00
	418.00	414.00	414.00	416.00
2X25	469.00	466.00	472.00	464.50
	509.00	500.00	502.00	499.00

Table 5.5 Results of GA Based Methods (Continued)

Problem Size	Makespan			
	SPCO-EAJ	SPCO-PAJ	TPCO-EAJ	TPCO-PAJ
3X11	90.00	89.50	86.00	89.00
	88.00	86.00	87.00	90.00
3X12	131.00	123.00	138.67	122.50
	125.00	120.00	120.00	118.00
3X13	134.00	121.33	124.50	121.50
	115.00	111.00	120.00	110.00
3X14	124.67	120.50	123.67	122.50
	133.00	128.00	135.00	130.00
3X15	160.33	142.33	143.50	139.00
	143.00	125.00	132.00	127.00
3X16	150.50	154.33	157.33	155.33
	176.00	164.00	198.00	164.00
3X17	170.50	171.33	174.00	171.67
	145.00	140.00	138.00	138.00
3X18	163.67	151.00	167.00	151.67
	164.00	159.00	168.00	162.00
3X19	202.00	194.00	213.50	194.00
	207.00	189.00	191.00	189.00
3X20	196.33	187.67	198.00	187.33
	210.00	192.00	205.00	192.00
3X21	218.50	210.00	228.00	214.33
	211.00	196.00	214.00	196.00
3X22	226.00	215.00	227.33	217.67
	208.00	197.00	207.00	197.00
3X23	237.67	221.67	235.00	224.33
	230.00	210.00	217.00	212.00
3X24	229.33	215.00	217.00	217.50
	219.00	208.00	209.00	207.00
3X25	214.33	206.00	213.00	204.00
	249.00	238.00	252.00	241.00

Table 5.5 Results of GA Based Methods (Continued)

Problem Size	Makespan			
	SPCO-EAJ	SPCO-PAJ	TPCO-EAJ	TPCO-PAJ
4X11	60.00	54.25	60.00	54.33
	63.00	61.00	60.00	61.00
4X12	83.25	75.00	85.00	75.00
	70.00	63.00	64.00	64.00
4X13	72.50	74.33	80.00	70.00
	83.00	81.00	86.00	81.00
4X14	83.00	75.75	85.00	74.00
	83.00	81.00	84.00	81.00
4X15	97.50	85.50	90.00	85.67
	93.00	87.00	90.00	84.00
4X16	92.66	83.00	86.00	86.67
	122.00	101.00	103.00	100.00
4X17	103.50	93.50	119.33	92.00
	114.00	92.00	96.00	91.00
4X18	108.50	112.00	122.25	112.50
	103.00	97.00	104.00	97.00
4X19	123.00	109.50	120.25	117.50
	108.00	109.00	116.00	107.00
4X20	115.00	105.33	131.25	108.50
	132.00	117.00	156.00	117.00
4X21	128.00	128.25	144.00	125.67
	138.00	135.00	137.00	137.00
4X22	129.50	123.00	133.75	123.50
	135.00	131.00	159.00	133.00
4X23	151.50	139.00	142.00	141.00
	147.00	139.00	142.00	142.00
4X24	153.50	143.50	156.50	145.00
	121.00	122.00	129.00	120.00
4X25	169.00	148.25	165.25	150.00
	168.00	147.00	180.00	154.00

Table 5.5 Results of GA Based Methods (Continued)

Problem Size	Makespan			
	SPCO-EAJ	SPCO-PAJ	TPCO-EAJ	TPCO-PAJ
5X11	58.67	49.20	49.80	48.60
	53.00	55.00	58.00	54.00
5X12	56.25	53.00	61.00	54.80
	60.00	48.00	56.00	48.00
5X13	70.20	62.60	63.60	65.25
	47.00	44.00	47.00	44.00
5X14	60.00	55.33	63.00	56.80
	60.00	51.00	54.00	55.00
5X15	64.40	52.80	56.50	56.67
	73.00	57.00	75.00	57.00
5X16	78.30	69.67	76.80	68.00
	64.00	53.00	60.00	54.00
5X17	79.00	67.33	70.60	69.40
	68.00	66.00	77.00	66.00
5X18	84.00	70.33	79.00	71.80
	81.00	73.00	84.00	80.00
5X19	77.20	66.67	77.00	65.67
	107.00	90.00	105.00	95.00
5X20	89.00	68.25	74.00	70.80
	66.00	57.00	60.00	56.00
5X21	99.40	87.25	98.67	93.60
	110.00	95.00	116.00	95.00
5X22	105.33	91.00	102.00	90.25
	85.00	87.00	95.00	88.00
5X23	120.00	88.00	100.67	87.75
	94.00	84.00	105.00	84.00
5X24	109.00	92.00	100.00	87.67
	114.00	106.00	116.00	108.00
5X25	118.00	95.67	117.50	94.75
	105.00	96.00	97.00	92.00

Table 5.5 Results of GA Based Methods (Continued)

Problem Size	Makespan			
	SPCO-EAJ	SPCO-PAJ	TPCO-EAJ	TPCO-PAJ
6X11	45.16	32.83	42.00	32.60
	28.00	30.00	34.00	30.00
6X12	53.80	42.50	56.50	41.50
	40.00	40.00	52.00	36.00
6X13	33.80	30.20	36.20	30.20
	37.00	33.00	33.00	32.00
6X14	54.00	42.67	46.80	43.25
	52.00	38.00	39.00	39.00
6X15	60.00	51.00	57.75	49.17
	52.00	42.00	46.00	39.00
6X16	59.00	50.75	58.00	51.50
	55.00	45.00	54.00	45.00
6X17	62.50	51.83	60.00	52.60
	49.00	43.00	44.00	42.00
6X18	56.00	54.83	66.67	53.17
	55.00	46.00	61.00	53.00
6X19	54.50	49.60	51.50	52.00
	58.00	55.00	75.00	54.00
6X20	84.00	74.50	77.67	71.50
	66.00	62.00	64.00	61.00
6X21	62.67	53.80	62.67	55.00
	67.00	57.00	65.00	55.00
6X22	75.00	62.20	73.75	62.60
	74.00	58.00	72.00	55.00
6X23	70.83	63.40	70.83	63.75
	83.00	72.00	88.00	78.00
6X24	80.00	69.83	71.50	66.33
	71.00	56.00	73.00	59.00
6X25	99.00	84.00	87.33	82.33
	91.00	85.00	106.00	81.00

Table 5.5 Results of GA Based Methods (Continued)

Problem Size	Makespan			
	SPCO-EAJ	SPCO-PAJ	TPCO-EAJ	TPCO-PAJ
7X11	24.85	25.20	24.00	24.25
	36.00	32.00	36.00	34.00
7X12	35.60	30.00	34.14	30.00
	35.00	30.00	30.00	30.00
7X13	42.71	30.00	38.71	30.00
	32.00	30.00	33.00	30.00
7X14	35.50	30.00	31.00	30.00
	39.00	33.00	43.00	32.00
7X15	37.00	30.00	41.57	30.00
	37.00	30.00	43.00	31.00
7X16	49.80	42.43	52.50	41.71
	33.00	32.00	36.00	30.00
7X17	49.80	42.43	57.71	45.29
	47.00	40.00	55.00	41.00
7X18	43.14	40.57	43.14	39.00
	48.00	40.00	47.00	39.00
7X19	61.85	47.50	60.00	48.33
	54.00	45.00	52.00	47.00
7X20	57.42	47.29	58.29	46.80
	59.00	50.00	68.00	52.00
7X21	74.00	45.00	49.25	46.29
	51.00	44.00	54.00	42.00
7X22	66.80	57.14	69.50	56.86
	64.00	55.00	58.00	55.00
7X23	57.42	51.43	62.50	52.00
	66.00	53.00	65.00	55.00
7X24	72.33	52.43	68.40	55.60
	55.00	49.00	60.00	51.00
7X25	63.85	55.00	60.00	56.71
	69.00	50.00	54.00	52.00

Table 5.5 Results of GA Based Methods (Continued)

Problem Size	Makespan			
	SPCO-EAJ	SPCO-PAJ	TPCO-EAJ	TPCO-PAJ
8X11	22.50	22.50	30.00	20.33
	27.00	30.00	27.00	27.00
8X12	35.20	25.17	33.62	30.00
	30.00	27.00	30.00	30.00
8X13	33.00	30.00	32.37	29.17
	34.00	30.00	38.00	31.00
8X14	39.25	32.13	39.12	30.13
	33.00	29.00	27.00	29.00
8X15	42.33	30.00	44.33	29.75
	39.00	32.00	45.00	30.00
8X16	30.00	30.00	30.00	29.29
	44.00	30.00	39.00	30.00
8X17	45.16	34.50	45.00	35.00
	31.00	30.00	31.00	30.00
8X18	41.71	31.43	45.50	36.00
	42.00	30.00	49.00	30.00
8X19	42.50	35.00	40.00	35.38
	43.00	31.00	40.00	32.00
8X20	50.66	35.38	40.50	32.67
	47.00	39.00	60.00	39.00
8X21	39.00	31.38	39.38	32.00
	41.00	38.00	41.00	34.00
8X22	48.25	37.14	49.00	39.00
	46.00	36.00	47.00	35.00
8X23	53.37	39.40	43.57	38.75
	40.00	33.00	39.00	32.00
8X24	50.25	36.83	48.00	36.88
	44.00	37.00	57.00	37.00
8X25	52.50	51.38	61.13	50.67
	57.00	36.00	54.00	36.00

Table 5.5 Results of GA Based Methods (Continued)

Problem Size	Makespan			
	SPCO-EAJ	SPCO-PAJ	TPCO-EAJ	TPCO-PAJ
9X11	23.28	23.29	24.75	24.75
	17.00	17.00	18.00	18.00
9X12	26.40	23.00	27.22	23.17
	27.00	25.00	30.00	30.00
9X13	29.67	26.78	30.00	23.50
	30.00	26.00	30.00	23.00
9X14	23.67	22.89	24.67	21.50
	30.00	30.00	29.00	30.00
9X15	30.00	25.88	30.00	23.86
	30.00	21.00	27.00	21.00
9X16	34.89	28.67	36.00	30.00
	25.00	19.00	29.00	25.00
9X17	51.22	30.00	40.11	31.22
	44.00	30.00	35.00	30.00
9X18	35.25	30.00	40.25	30.00
	40.00	30.00	45.00	30.00
9X19	33.12	34.22	45.56	32.00
	47.00	33.00	38.00	36.00
9X20	33.25	31.29	46.50	32.29
	34.00	30.00	46.00	31.00
9X21	38.00	40.14	56.33	37.00
	45.00	30.00	46.00	31.00
9X22	48.50	41.33	49.80	46.67
	47.00	33.00	41.00	35.00
9X23	39.00	34.67	44.80	32.33
	45.00	30.00	41.00	30.00
9X24	57.78	40.56	48.89	39.00
	37.00	32.00	34.00	31.00
9X25	32.83	30.00	36.44	30.22
	42.00	32.00	43.00	33.00

Table 5.5 Results of GA Based Methods (Continued)

Problem Size	Makespan			
	SPCO-EAJ	SPCO-PAJ	TPCO-EAJ	TPCO-PAJ
10X11	12.11	12.11	14.40	14.40
	20.00	20.00	17.00	20.00
10X12	19.42	19.43	19.83	19.83
	21.00	18.00	17.00	22.00
10X13	17.42	21.33	19.67	20.80
	18.00	17.00	18.00	15.00
10X14	25.67	24.20	29.80	25.17
	28.00	27.00	26.00	23.00
10X15	26.90	19.56	21.60	20.44
	30.00	26.00	30.00	24.00
10X16	27.10	24.30	22.20	20.60
	24.00	20.00	30.00	24.00
10X17	36.00	30.00	37.20	29.50
	23.00	23.00	21.00	23.00
10X18	44.00	30.30	41.00	31.67
	43.00	30.00	41.00	30.00
10X19	43.90	30.00	35.00	30.00
	42.00	30.00	44.00	30.00
10X20	35.00	32.60	41.67	30.22
	30.00	33.00	30.00	30.00
10X21	42.42	30.00	41.20	29.25
	36.00	30.00	36.00	30.00
10X22	38.42	30.00	43.33	30.00
	30.00	28.00	35.00	30.00
10X23	35.50	30.00	33.60	30.00
	35.00	30.00	30.00	29.00
10X24	37.00	30.00	31.13	29.50
	38.00	30.00	31.00	30.00
10X25	37.50	32.00	40.75	30.60
	42.00	30.00	35.00	30.00

The different hypotheses of this model are listed below.

Factor: Problem Size(A)

H0: The makespan value does not significantly vary depending on the size of the problem.

H1: The makespan value varies significantly depending on the size of the problem.

Factor: Crossover Method(B)

HO: The makespan value does not significantly differ between the crossover methods.

H1: The makespan value of the crossover methods differs significantly from one another.

Interaction: Problem Size (A) X Crossover Method (B)

HO: The makespan value of the various pairings of interaction terms of the problem size and crossover method does not significantly differ from one another.

H1: The makespan value of the various pairings of interaction terms of the problem size and crossover method differs significantly.

Factor: Job Allocation Method(C)

HO: The makespan value of the various job allocation methods does not significantly differ from one another.

H1: The makespan value of the various job allocation methods varies significantly.

Interaction: Problem Size (A) X Job Allocation Method (C)

HO: The makespan value does not significantly differ between various pairings of interaction factors related to the problem size and the job allocation method.

H1: The makespan value of various pairs of interaction terms pertaining to problem size and job allocation method varies significantly.

Interaction: Crossover Method (B) X Job Allocation Method (C)

HO: The makespan value of the various pairs of crossover method and job allocation method interaction terms does not significantly differ from one another.

H1: The makespan value of the various pairings of interaction terms in the crossover method and job allocation method differs significantly.

Interaction: Problem Size (A) X Crossover method (B) X Job Allocation Method (C)

HO: The makespan value does not significantly differ between various combinations of the interaction terms of problem size, crossover method, and job allocation method.

H1: The makespan value significantly differs between various combinations of the interaction terms of problem size, crossover method, and job allocation method.

Table 5.6 displays the outcomes of the relevant ANOVA model.

These are the hypotheses for which the results are noteworthy.

Factor "Problem Size (A)":

The calculated F ratio for the factor "Problem Size (A)" in Table 5.6 is 288.8273 at a significance level of 0.05, which is higher than the corresponding table F value of 1 for (134, 540) degrees of freedom. Consequently, the alternative hypothesis is accepted. This suggests that there were considerable differences in the problem sizes with regard to makespan.

Table 5.6 Results of ANOVA

Source of Variation	Sum of squares	Degrees of freedom	Mean sum of squares	$C_{alculated}$	F_{table} at $\alpha=0.05$	Inference
A (Problem Size)	1.008905×10^7	134	752914.000000	288.82730	1.00	Significant
B (Crossover Method)	4.793457	1	4.7934570	0.01839	3.84	Insignificant
AB	1940.207000	134	14.479150	0.05554	1.00	Insignificant
C (Job Allocation Method)	14520.950000	1	14520.950000	55.70418	3.84	Significant
AC	5187.055000	134	38.709360	0.14849	1.00	Insignificant
BC	2.562500	1	2.562500	0.00983	3.84	Insignificant
ABC	1787.438000	134	13.339090	0.05117	1.00	Insignificant
Error	140767.000000	540	260.679600			
Total	1.025326×10^7	1079				

Factor "Job Allocation Method" (C):

The factor "Job Allocation Method (C)" in Table 5.6 has a computed F ratio of 55.70418, which is more than the table F value of 3.84 for (1, 540) degrees of freedom at a significance level of 0.05. As a result, the related alternative hypothesis is approved. This indicates that there are notable variations in the makespan between the job allocation methods.

The results of the ANOVA show that there are notable differences in the makespan between the various job allocation methods. The equal number of job allocation to the machines has a mean makespan of 101.6658, whereas the proportionate number of job allocation to the machines has a mean makespan of 94.13222, which indicates that the latter is superior.

Furthermore, it has been noted that the makespan of various problem sizes varies significantly. This result provides even more evidence for the highly significant differences in makespan across the job allocation methods.

It is found that, in terms of makespan, there is no significant difference between the single point and two-point crossover methods. Therefore, any of these two crossover methods may be chosen and put into practice. In comparison to the GA-based heuristic with two-point crossover method paired with proportionate job allocation method, which has a mean makespan of 94.24752, the heuristic with single-point crossover method and proportionate job allocation method has a mean makespan of 94.01693, which is lesser.

The GA based heuristic with single point crossover approach is advised in light of the previously discussed points. This method generates the initial population by allocating jobs to the machines proportionately based on their speeds.

REVIEW QUESTIONS

1. What is GA based heuristic?
2. Give the skeleton of GA based algorithm.
3. List and explain the factors affecting the performance of the GA based algorithm applied to minimize the makespan of scheduling jobs on uniform parallel machines.
4. Explain the single point crossover method applied to minimize the makespan of scheduling jobs on uniform parallel machines.
5. What are proposed GA based heuristics to minimize the makespan of scheduling jobs on uniform parallel machines?
6. Explain the steps of the GA based heuristic with single-point crossover method and equal number of jobs allocation method.
7. Explain the steps of GA based heuristic with two-point crossover method and equal number of jobs allocation method.
8. Explain the steps of ga based heuristic with single point crossover method and proportionate number of jobs allocation method
9. Explain the steps of ga based heuristic with two-point crossover method and proportionate number of jobs allocation method.
10. Discuss the details of the complete factorial experiment to compare different GA based heuristics to minimize the makespan of scheduling jobs on uniform parallel machines.

6 COMPARISON OF SIMULATED ANNEALING ALGORITHM SA₂ AND BEST GA BASED HEURISTIC SPCO-PAJ TO MINIMIZE MAKESPAN IN SINGLE MACHINE SCHEDULING PROBLEM WITH UNIFORM PARALLEL MACHINES

6.1 INTRODUCTION

Chapter 4 presents three distinct simulated annealing algorithms, one of which is recommended to minimize the makespan of the uniform parallel machine single machine scheduling problem. Chapter 5 presents four distinct GA-based algorithms, one of which is recommended to minimize the makespan of the uniform parallel machine single machine scheduling problem. The best algorithms recommended in Chapters 4 and 6 are compared in this chapter.

6.2 COMPARISON OF BEST ALGORITHMS OF SIMULATED ANNEALING ALGORITHM AND GA BASED HEURISTIC

In order to minimize the makespan of the single machine scheduling problem with uniform parallel machines, the simulated annealing algorithm SA2 is proposed in Chapter 4. The GA based heuristic with single-point crossover method is proposed in Chapter 5 and generates the initial population by allocating jobs to the machines proportionately based on their speeds.

This chapter compares the performance of the two algorithms indicated above using the same sets of data (replication 1 and replication 2) as shown in Appendices 1 and 2, respectively, which are used in Chapters 4 and 5.

To compare the algorithms, a complete factorial experiment with two replications is used in the experimental design. The number of jobs in this experiment ranges from 11 to 25, while the number of machines varies from 2 to 10. Data on processing times have been randomly generated by assuming the speed of 1 for machine-1, the speed of 2 for machine-2,... and the speed of m for machine-m for each combination of the number of uniform parallel machines and the number of jobs which are to be scheduled in them. Table 6.1 provides an overview of the makespan values and mean percent deviation obtained from the two algorithms.

In this comparison, the two algorithms, namely SA2 and SPCO-PAJ, form the treatments of the factor "Algorithm" (Factor B), and the problems presented in Appendices 1 and 2 represent the treatments of the factor "problem Size" (Factor A).

Table 6.1 Results of Comparison of SA_2 and SPCO-PAJ

Problem Size	Makespan	
	SA_2	SPCO-PAJ
2X11	199.00	200.00
	179.00	177.00
2X12	201.50	201.50
	193.00	193.00
2X13	256.00	254.50
	205.00	202.00
2X14	225.00	220.50
	280.00	274.00
2X15	338.00	338.50
	264.00	264.00
2X16	287.00	284.50
	284.00	286.00
2X17	333.00	330.00
	323.00	322.00
2X18	376.50	375.00
	277.00	277.00
2X19	320.50	319.00
	358.00	357.00
2X20	300.00	299.00
	445.00	444.00
2X21	407.00	407.00
	312.00	310.00
2X22	408.00	407.00
	409.00	407.00
2X23	399.50	399.00
	391.00	391.00
2X24	361.00	361.00
	415.00	414.00
2X25	466.50	466.00
	499.00	500.00

Table 6.1 Results of Comparison of SA$_2$ and SPCO-PAJ (Continued)

Problem Size	Makespan	
	SA$_2$	SPCO-PAJ
3X11	86.00	89.50
	86.00	86.00
3X12	122.00	123.00
	120.00	120.00
3X13	127.00	121.33
	110.00	111.00
3X14	121.50	120.50
	131.00	128.00
3X15	144.00	142.33
	126.00	125.00
3X16	150.00	154.33
	165.00	164.00
3X17	168.50	171.33
	138.00	140.00
3X18	152.00	151.00
	164.00	159.00
3X19	199.00	194.00
	187.00	189.00
3X20	189.00	187.67
	189.00	192.00
3X21	214.00	210.00
	200.00	196.00
3X22	218.00	215.00
	195.00	197.00
3X23	221.00	221.67
	210.00	210.00
3X24	215.00	215.00
	205.00	208.00
3X25	206.00	206.00
	237.00	238.00

Table 6.1 Results of Comparison of SA₂ and SPCO-PAJ (Continued)

Problem Size	Makespan	
	SA₂	SPCO-PAJ
4X11	59.30	54.25
	61.00	61.00
4X12	78.00	75.00
	64.00	63.00
4X13	69.00	74.33
	81.00	81.00
4X14	76.80	75.75
	76.00	81.00
4X15	86.70	85.50
	84.00	87.00
4X16	84.30	83.00
	99.00	101.00
4X17	93.00	93.50
	93.00	92.00
4X18	111.00	112.00
	95.00	97.00
4X19	107.00	109.50
	104.00	109.00
4X20	105.50	105.33
	115.00	117.00
4X21	127.50	128.25
	135.00	135.00
4X22	121.70	123.00
	133.00	131.00
4X23	131.80	139.00
	140.00	139.00
4X24	140.00	143.50
	119.00	122.00
4X25	149.30	148.25
	147.00	147.00

Table 6.1 Results of Comparison of SA₂ and SPCO-PAJ (Continued)

Problem Size	Makespan	
	SA₂	SPCO-PAJ
5X11	44.40	49.20
	51.00	55.00
5X12	51.50	53.00
	46.00	48.00
5X13	57.00	62.60
	43.00	44.00
5X14	52.00	55.33
	48.00	51.00
5X15	53.40	52.80
	56.00	57.00
5X16	68.50	69.67
	57.00	53.00
5X17	68.00	67.33
	64.00	66.00
5X18	67.40	70.33
	71.00	73.00
5X19	65.50	66.67
	91.00	90.00
5X20	67.80	68.25
	57.00	57.00
5X21	87.50	87.25
	91.00	95.00
5X22	88.00	91.00
	82.00	87.00
5X23	87.00	88.00
	85.00	84.00
5X24	87.40	92.00
	103.00	106.00
5X25	92.50	95.67
	94.00	96.00

Table 6.1 Results of Comparison of SA$_2$ and SPCO-PAJ (Continued)

Problem Size	Makespan	
	SA$_2$	SPCO-PAJ
6X11	32.20	32.83
	26.00	30.00
6X12	36.50	42.50
	35.00	40.00
6X13	30.00	30.20
	32.00	33.00
6X14	41.00	42.67
	36.00	38.00
6X15	45.80	51.00
	35.00	42.00
6X16	46.60	50.75
	44.00	45.00
6X17	51.30	51.83
	39.00	43.00
6X18	51.30	54.83
	48.00	46.00
6X19	45.80	49.60
	49.00	55.00
6X20	61.30	74.50
	53.00	62.00
6X21	51.50	53.80
	54.00	57.00
6X22	61.80	62.20
	55.00	58.00
6X23	62.00	63.40
	72.00	72.00
6X24	63.00	69.83
	57.00	56.00
6X25	73.70	84.00
	74.00	85.00

Table 6.1 Results of Comparison of SA$_2$ and SPCO-PAJ (Continued)

Problem Size	Makespan	
	SA$_2$	SPCO-PAJ
7X11	19.30	25.20
	27.00	32.00
7X12	25.40	30.00
	26.00	30.00
7X13	27.80	30.00
	26.00	30.00
7X14	27.90	30.00
	30.00	33.00
7X15	29.50	30.00
	29.00	30.00
7X16	37.70	42.43
	30.00	32.00
7X17	39.00	42.43
	37.00	40.00
7X18	34.00	40.57
	33.00	40.00
7X19	46.40	47.50
	45.00	45.00
7X20	42.20	47.29
	46.00	50.00
7X21	42.50	45.00
	42.00	44.00
7X22	48.30	57.14
	49.00	55.00
7X23	47.00	51.43
	51.00	53.00
7X24	51.60	52.43
	49.00	49.00
7X25	49.30	55.00
	45.00	50.00

Table 6.1 Results of Comparison of SA$_2$ and SPCO-PAJ (Continued)

Problem Size	Makespan	
	SA$_2$	SPCO-PAJ
8X11	18.30	22.50
	21.00	30.00
8X12	23.90	25.17
	21.00	27.00
8X13	21.60	30.00
	25.00	30.00
8X14	26.00	32.13
	21.00	29.00
8X15	27.00	30.00
	26.00	32.00
8X16	23.00	30.00
	26.00	30.00
8X17	30.00	34.50
	25.00	30.00
8X18	31.60	31.43
	26.00	30.00
8X19	30.00	35.00
	34.00	31.00
8X20	30.80	35.38
	32.00	39.00
8X21	30.00	31.38
	33.00	38.00
8X22	33.30	37.14
	30.00	36.00
8X23	34.80	39.40
	35.00	33.00
8X24	34.20	36.83
	35.00	37.00
8X25	45.00	51.38
	12.00	36.00

Table 6.1 Results of Comparison of SA₂ and SPCO-PAJ (Continued)

Problem Size	Makespan	
	SA₂	SPCO-PAJ
9X11	16.30	23.29
	12.00	17.00
9X12	16.30	23.00
	18.00	25.00
9X13	17.60	26.78
	19.00	26.00
9X14	17.50	22.89
	19.00	30.00
9X15	18.50	25.88
	18.00	21.00
9X16	21.30	28.67
	16.00	19.00
9X17	25.80	30.00
	24.00	30.00
9X18	27.30	30.00
	23.00	30.00
9X19	27.50	34.22
	29.00	33.00
9X20	28.30	31.29
	29.00	30.00
9X21	29.70	40.14
	28.00	30.00
9X22	33.00	41.33
	29.00	33.00
9X23	31.40	34.67
	27.00	30.00
9X24	33.90	40.56
	29.00	32.00
9X25	25.70	30.00
	29.00	32.00

Table 6.1 Results of Comparison of SA$_2$ and SPCO-PAJ (Continued)

Problem Size	Makespan	
	SA$_2$	SPCO-PAJ
10X11	10.60	12.11
	12.00	20.00
10X12	13.70	19.43
	13.00	18.00
10X13	15.00	21.33
	12.00	17.00
10X14	16.30	24.20
	17.00	27.00
10X15	16.00	19.56
	16.00	26.00
10X16	15.80	24.30
	17.00	20.00
10X17	19.80	30.00
	16.00	23.00
10X18	21.80	30.30
	21.00	30.00
10X19	23.40	30.00
	22.00	30.00
10X20	24.30	32.60
	22.00	33.00
10X21	26.10	30.00
	22.00	30.00
10X22	23.00	30.00
	22.00	28.00
10X23	24.20	30.00
	21.00	30.00
10X24	23.10	30.00
	23.00	30.00
10X25	27.00	32.00
	25.00	30.00

The whole factorial experiment model, which was utilized to examine the data in Table 6.1, is displayed below.

$$Y_{ijk} = \mu + P_i + A_j + PA_{ij} + e_{ijk}$$

where,

- For the ith problem size (Factor A) and the jth treatment of the method (Factor B), Y_{ijk} is the makespan of the kth replication.

- ○ μ be the total mean.
- ○ The impact of Factor A's i^{th} treatment on the makespan is represented by the letter A_i.
- ○ The impact of Factor B's j^{th} treatment on the makespan is denoted by B_j.
- ○ The impact of Factor A's i^{th} treatment and Factor B's j^{th} treatment on the makespan is represented by the expression AB^{ij}.
- ○ The random error connected to the mean of the kth replication with respect to the ith treatment of Factor A and the jth treatment of Factor B is called e_{ijk}.

The hypotheses of this experiment are presented below.

Factor A (Problem Size)

> H0: The mean makespan values of the problems do not significantly differ from one another.
>
> H1: For at least one pair of problems, there is a significant difference between the mean makespan values of the problems.

Factor B (Algorithm)

> H0: In terms of the mean makespan values, there is no significant difference between the GA-based heuristic SPCO-PAJ and the simulated annealing algorithm SA2.
>
> H1: The makespan values of the GA-based heuristic SPCO-PAJ and the simulated annealing algorithm SA2 differ significantly.

Factor AB (Problem Size X Algorithm)

> H0: In terms of the mean makespan values, there is no visible difference between the interaction terms of Factor A and Factor B.
>
> H1: The mean makespan values show a substantial difference between the interaction terms of Factor A and Factor B.

Table 6.2 shows the results of this ANOVA.

Table 6.2 Results of ANOVA

Source of Variation	Sum of squares	Degrees of freedom	Mean sum of squares	$F_{calculated}$	F_{table} at $\alpha=0.05$	Inference
A (Problem Size)	5177255.0	134	38636.23000	157.2520	1.00	Reject Ho
B (Best Algorithm)	1116.5	1	1116.50000	4.5442	3.84	Reject Ho
AB	1510.5	134	11.27239	0.0459	1.00	Accept Ho
Error	66338.0	270	245.69630			
Total	5246220.0	539				

Inference

Factor A (Problem Size): At a significance level of 0.05, the computed F ratio of the factor "Problem Size" is 157.25, which is greater than the table F ratio of 1. As a result, the null hypothesis about this factor is rejected. This indicates that the problem sizes varied significantly in terms of the makespan values.

Factor B (Algorithm): At a significance level of 0.05, the estimated F ratio of the factor "Algorithm" is 4.5442, which is greater than the F ratio of 3.84 in the table. As a result, the null hypothesis about this factor is rejected. This indicates that, in terms of makespan values, there is a substantial difference between the GA-based heuristic SPCO-PAJ and the simulated annealing algorithm SA2.

Interaction AB: At a significance level of 0.05, the calculated F ratio of the interaction terms is 0.0459, which is less than the table F ratio of 1. The null hypothesis with regard to this factor is therefore accepted. This indicates that, in terms of the makespan values, there is no significant difference between the interaction terms of Problem Size and Algorithm.

Their mean makespan values are compared because it has been demonstrated that there is a considerable difference between the GA-based heuristic SPCO-PAJ and the simulated annealing algorithm SA2. The simulated annealing algorithm SA2 and the GA-based heuristic SPCO-PAJ have mean makespan values of 91.1 and 94.01693, respectively.

The simulated annealing algorithm SA2 is recommended to minimize the makespan of the single machine scheduling problem with uniform parallel machines because it has the lowest mean makespan.

REVIEW QUESTIONS

1. Give the experimental design (Complete factorial experiment) to compare the best SA algorithm and bets GA algorithm.

APPENDIX 1 DATA ON PROCESSING TIMES OF JOBS IN REPLICATION 1

The processing times of the jobs on machine 1 in replication 1 are displayed in this appendix for the numbers of machines 2, 3, 4, 5, 6, 7, 8, 9, and 10, correspondingly, from Table A.1.1 to Table A.1.9. There are 11 to 25 jobs in each table.

Let,

n be the number of jobs

m be the number of machines

s_i be the speed of the machine i, where i = 1, 2,3, ..., m.

t_{1j} be the processing time of the job j on the machine 1, where j = 1, 2, 3, ..., n.

The following formula provides the processing times of a given job j on the machines ranging from 2 to m.

$t_{ij} = t_{1j}/s_i$, where varies from 2 to m.

Therefore, the above equation may be used to calculate the processing time of a job on the other machines if the processing time of the job on machine 1 is known. For each job, the processing time on machine 1 alone is provided in this appendix. The programme itself will use the above formula to calculate each job's processing time on the other machine.

Table A.1.1 Processing Times of Jobs on Machine 1 When the Number of Machines is 2

Problem Size	Job Number												
	1	2	3	4	5	6	7	8	9	10	11	12	13
	14	15	16	17	18	19	20	21	22	23	24	25	
2X11	91	57	30	70	72	30	39	30	67	30	81		
2X12	30	59	92	30	59	72	36	54	30	55	56	30	
2X13	66	40	88	59	47	48	41	87	30	90	69	68	30
2X14	30	30	42	94	50	67	30	93	30	30	30	75	30
	30												
2X15	82	86	54	82	96	83	78	94	37	51	30	42	84
	64	49											
2X16	57	30	63	32	54	72	58	99	30	97	38	30	30
	77	30	54										
2X17	80	83	30	46	73	30	44	70	30	44	31	31	93
	90	39	91	84									
2X18	59	94	30	44	81	30	38	76	95	58	57	72	85
	90	83	44	38	49								
2X19	98	38	30	34	30	63	30	30	79	67	75	30	47
	47	30	30	80	30	88							
2X20	52	30	51	36	30	54	30	93	30	30	69	30	95
	30	30	40	30	63	40	33						
2X21	30	30	58	30	51	52	30	92	75	46	68	30	48
	74	76	43	67	94	30	94	99					
2X22	43	93	43	61	96	47	67	58	30	30	78	30	30
	84	67	69	30	61	30	41	54	77				
2X23	38	68	30	61	72	60	78	51	39	72	30	50	30
	30	47	67	76	61	30	30	49	44	82			
2X24	32	30	35	40	30	41	36	56	31	68	61	89	30
	30	30	56	30	60	30	30	30	43	78	86		
2X25	50	84	41	30	96	30	78	46	30	97	30	80	30
	30	65	75	99	36	85	77	30	56	30	30	55	

Table A.1.2 Processing Times of Jobs on Machine 1 When the Number of Machines is 3

Problem Size	Job Number												
	1	2	3	4	5	6	7	8	9	10	11	12	13
	14	15	16	17	18	19	20	21	22	23	24	25	
3X11	30	62	51	47	34	45	30	30	57	57	56		
3X12	34	72	72	99	31	30	66	71	76	30	68	66	
3X13	47	46	38	60	94	30	65	69	30	89	47	65	30
3X14	70	55	75	37	59	65	45	55	45	30	35	40	46
	62												
3X15	88	30	52	93	93	65	30	30	53	94	30	30	30
	57	51											
3X16	90	30	68	44	53	84	30	68	30	78	99	48	30
	78	30	30										
3X17	97	77	41	52	50	36	34	90	30	34	98	49	30
	64	83	88	34									
3X18	88	67	30	48	56	98	41	30	71	51	30	41	44
	80	30	30	30	30								
3X19	92	30	56	30	74	93	48	87	30	62	31	95	59
	90	40	30	33	76	91							
3X20	97	89	30	41	30	30	85	30	96	65	30	99	30
	77	51	82	30	43	30	37						
3X21	89	76	54	67	84	85	68	30	30	50	74	33	57
	30	57	85	30	54	68	87	43					
3X22	82	86	30	76	30	30	70	45	30	47	58	88	84
	32	95	30	58	90	30	61	61	62				
3X23	30	93	30	94	68	81	30	30	49	50	87	48	66
	53	41	30	57	56	30	99	47	67	80			
3X24	30	57	42	49	87	69	30	41	71	60	48	33	79
	30	79	87	30	30	30	62	48	87	74	30		
3X25	30	41	90	57	53	45	30	30	51	30	43	61	30
	30	54	30	73	30	61	30	95	30	58	54	84	

Table A.1.3 Processing Times of Jobs on Machine 1 When the Number of Machines is 4

Problem Size	Job Number												
	1	2	3	4	5	6	7	8	9	10	11	12	13
	14	15	16	17	18	19	20	21	22	23	24	25	
4X11	51	54	73	30	50	71	30	30	30	30	60		
4X12	75	34	54	96	82	33	30	46	33	98	92	39	
4X13	31	30	66	30	34	57	30	77	30	47	93	87	31
4X14	30	79	88	30	30	30	30	34	68	30	50	81	81
	52												
4X15	30	49	48	69	73	30	45	30	49	64	30	90	51
	92	69											
4X16	31	30	65	83	30	30	47	67	92	30	45	66	37
	68	30	44										
4X17	30	90	30	73	30	47	30	35	30	45	55	90	30
	30	67	96	84									
4X18	78	33	30	98	30	36	99	30	93	34	30	71	34
	65	85	78	61	64								
4X19	30	46	73	95	39	30	90	30	30	56	54	72	96
	37	44	30	68	30	83							
4X20	48	68	91	65	31	30	98	47	30	58	86	35	30
	63	35	30	69	43	54	30						
4X21	79	30	78	40	95	52	86	65	30	30	37	34	56
	98	30	34	92	30	84	90	46					
4X22	85	30	72	46	47	30	60	75	30	30	88	30	41
	92	30	35	38	36	93	70	30	87				
4X23	30	46	81	95	30	30	37	34	30	77	94	91	76
	41	50	30	41	91	90	38	74	72	32			
4X24	49	61	74	82	38	72	31	65	50	74	37	39	76
	73	30	33	37	94	86	30	37	99	81	30		
4X25	83	83	38	99	60	89	32	30	30	30	62	91	37
	43	64	82	30	57	30	74	30	87	56	79	41	

Table A.1.4 Processing Times of Jobs on Machine 1 When the Number of Machines is 5

Problem Size	Job Number												
	1	2	3	4	5	6	7	8	9	10	11	12	13
	14	15	16	17	18	19	20	21	22	23	24	25	
5X11	74	75	78	71	34	84	30	30	30	30	89		
5X12	73	30	51	77	49	30	78	66	99	53	98	31	
5X13	33	91	89	70	30	33	72	30	88	84	85	30	75
5X14	45	44	57	30	52	30	30	82	74	92	52	52	54
	30												
5X15	83	57	30	30	30	55	30	62	30	57	30	85	30
	90	30											
5X16	75	30	34	77	83	55	86	95	35	30	30	93	86
	44	74	30										
5X17	30	43	87	74	30	46	93	39	30	62	33	77	42
	50	37	84	90									
5X18	50	90	30	63	36	30	46	30	30	30	91	86	92
	30	40	35	81	63								
5X19	39	40	34	75	30	30	48	30	30	81	30	95	30
	55	30	96	30	71	30							
5X20	37	31	30	71	30	30	59	49	45	30	76	30	30
	88	30	82	94	61	30	31						
5X21	30	30	30	63	65	50	95	56	30	97	68	30	87
	58	93	41	57	69	30	99	87					
5X22	76	45	43	49	77	30	90	89	39	30	73	39	30
	30	58	30	67	34	93	55	91	88				
5X23	88	66	50	30	74	57	53	30	43	88	76	30	30
	89	30	30	30	30	48	98	75	78	30			
5X24	72	35	56	30	69	30	83	80	30	73	91	30	30
	72	30	30	92	78	30	35	38	83	30	30		
5X25	44	37	48	93	90	96	30	30	68	39	70	89	63
	44	30	41	37	57	90	58	30	30	39	49	53	

Table A.1.5 Processing Times of Jobs on Machine 1 When the Number of Machines is 6

Problem Size	Job Number												
	1	2	3	4	5	6	7	8	9	10	11	12	13
	14	15	16	17	18	19	20	21	22	23	24	25	
6X11	51	73	30	30	86	84	65	30	30	30	98		
6X12	42	73	68	88	30	30	86	41	56	83	30	83	
6X13	30	30	30	30	30	60	78	30	30	30	91	30	48
6X14	58	67	53	74	30	55	50	30	82	47	99	30	42
	70												
6X15	30	30	87	80	98	30	30	30	30	91	62	77	94
	30	73											
6X16	56	97	30	74	30	44	95	32	49	40	85	62	88
	59	45	58										
6X17	30	54	74	50	30	73	93	90	30	30	75	30	57
	66	73	30	79									
6X18	54	86	99	53	54	30	71	67	46	69	30	60	30
	87	30	40	48	58								
6X19	30	59	30	30	30	57	48	30	55	88	30	30	75
	39	42	68	30	97	35							
6X20	30	53	52	30	56	76	99	49	38	69	30	68	96
	77	83	88	30	94	65	66						
6X21	30	30	30	49	30	30	30	98	30	96	83	40	30
	87	38	30	30	30	57	30	98					
6X22	76	75	91	30	30	82	30	30	78	44	30	43	30
	30	71	83	30	40	74	39	89	72				
6X23	30	83	33	30	81	91	96	94	30	93	36	64	54
	30	59	30	30	30	56	99	30	30	30			
6X24	30	30	30	82	55	72	59	52	30	34	30	57	30
	30	30	69	71	71	91	38	74	61	56	68		
6X25	86	52	71	31	97	81	33	31	62	30	86	66	30
	99	42	58	71	66	30	94	49	30	42	94	30	

Table A.1.6 Processing Times of Jobs on Machine 1 When the Number of Machines is 7

Problem Size	Job Number												
	1	2	3	4	5	6	7	8	9	10	11	12	13
	14	15	16	17	18	19	20	21	22	23	24	25	
7X11	37	66	30	30	37	32	30	78	30	52	30		
7X12	30	49	49	86	30	30	30	30	60	40	67	99	
7X13	49	30	70	57	30	51	30	38	78	72	37	30	95
7X14	48	30	30	86	89	53	30	30	30	41	94	30	30
	30												
7X15	30	30	59	36	81	30	37	52	30	48	30	99	30
	65	30											
7X16	30	98	79	30	30	30	49	31	76	81	88	75	82
	76	90	33										
7X17	30	81	56	30	88	42	96	54	30	39	87	58	89
	86	68	71	30									
7X18	39	74	30	68	30	38	50	40	62	30	30	39	30
	93	38	67	58	44								
7X19	99	30	98	89	30	54	30	30	80	86	30	70	96
	30	80	48	88	78	44							
7X20	30	62	47	30	60	91	65	63	55	88	51	91	30
	30	66	30	78	32	30	82						
7X21	30	61	60	30	66	49	31	30	30	69	76	89	96
	30	66	30	74	30	30	68	40					
7X22	84	30	93	51	30	30	85	82	30	30	59	92	30
	42	54	94	66	30	87	72	30	85				
7X23	99	56	62	60	87	32	38	43	30	62	30	42	75
	30	75	83	30	30	30	80	30	30	98			
7X24	81	52	89	30	93	50	30	45	55	30	41	33	80
	90	30	30	73	30	72	62	75	30	30	98		
7X25	45	35	67	36	30	76	99	97	97	34	61	32	54
	30	43	30	64	30	73	60	36	30	30	79	47	

Table A.1.7 Processing Times of Jobs on Machine 1 When the Number of Machines is 8

Problem Size	Job Number												
	1	2	3	4	5	6	7	8	9	10	11	12	13
	14	15	16	17	18	19	20	21	22	23	24	25	
8X11	32	30	90	82	30	34	70	38	73	43	30		
8X12	49	93	38	30	87	33	88	88	63	30	83	74	
8X13	30	85	52	30	61	47	34	85	64	30	60	36	45
8X14	82	30	44	30	82	70	56	92	71	69	87	41	30
	30												
8X15	94	30	30	73	76	85	30	48	30	60	84	44	30
	71	75											
8X16	30	30	78	30	55	67	67	30	30	34	43	67	30
	30	30	60										
8X17	30	94	30	32	30	42	91	83	60	64	69	51	82
	50	83	30	74									
8X18	94	92	98	30	82	89	39	30	43	58	30	38	82
	30	55	73	45	43								
8X19	50	30	88	30	73	55	31	82	60	30	68	73	30
	55	79	40	32	30	47							
8X20	73	30	68	53	30	30	30	80	30	89	30	42	30
	30	30	86	30	39	92	81						
8X21	71	30	30	36	44	59	30	85	34	30	65	30	30
	67	30	30	30	30	30	91	87					
8X22	30	67	91	91	41	32	57	30	67	30	30	43	36
	39	30	30	68	30	96	31	60	65				
8X23	30	30	30	86	79	46	31	63	73	30	72	81	30
	30	82	30	50	35	31	34	30	94	30			
8X24	80	87	98	30	30	30	30	30	30	81	30	80	30
	30	84	30	30	30	40	30	63	30	65	30		
8X25	30	97	51	30	66	30	30	79	68	47	91	63	30
	85	41	50	58	30	69	47	54	98	92	78	84	

Table A.1.8 Processing Times of Jobs on Machine 1 When the Number of Machines is 9

Problem Size	Job Number												
	1	2	3	4	5	6	7	8	9	10	11	12	13
	14	15	16	17	18	19	20	21	22	23	24	25	
9X11	57	30	49	81	96	36	30	30	84	30	87		
9X12	30	66	81	30	73	30	54	58	46	74	33	68	
9X13	86	30	30	42	58	30	30	68	82	43	73	82	30
9X14	43	30	30	92	62	72	30	80	61	30	31	34	30
	30												
9X15	30	30	48	89	30	43	30	33	90	45	93	30	44
	30	30											
9X16	30	87	30	30	44	47	30	30	30	78	94	53	78
	45	84	35										
9X17	30	76	73	50	37	65	83	30	78	59	73	55	56
	59	96	38	69									
9X18	83	51	66	86	76	31	80	30	67	46	90	33	30
	45	82	30	94	70								
9X19	92	44	95	91	45	72	71	30	96	58	30	30	43
	30	30	30	64	97	30							
9X20	77	63	42	40	30	90	92	30	30	48	68	70	46
	64	92	30	53	50	37	87						
9X21	30	30	75	48	92	65	53	30	49	99	59	90	37
	72	53	90	30	49	48	55	92					
9X22	69	77	79	65	30	37	90	84	38	85	59	60	82
	55	66	30	37	99	36	30	77	97				
9X23	73	50	88	86	30	92	30	30	30	75	31	55	54
	30	49	30	67	41	30	83	90	93	30			
9X24	71	95	49	30	30	46	61	93	86	83	32	62	56
	65	38	30	30	78	76	90	44	37	60	77		
9X25	30	30	54	55	30	44	35	30	39	30	30	30	53
	46	30	30	72	42	30	30	30	39	94	30	79	

Table A.1.9 Processing Times of Jobs on Machine 1 When the Number of Machines is 10

Problem Size	Job Number												
	1	2	3	4	5	6	7	8	9	10	11	12	13
	14	15	16	17	18	19	20	21	22	23	24	25	
10X11	30	30	35	44	44	79	30	50	30	30	30		
10X12	69	38	53	59	30	30	66	30	83	95	36	30	
10X13	70	30	44	92	62	74	69	30	44	30	30	39	64
10X14	77	44	54	54	57	60	60	30	38	54	93	91	44
	59												
10X15	76	30	81	34	30	57	30	30	66	88	30	58	75
	46	30											
10X16	83	33	30	54	30	30	34	49	57	46	37	30	30
	86	58	49										
10X17	45	82	76	30	49	30	31	91	36	98	30	98	30
	30	30	84	72									
10X18	30	34	97	65	87	65	39	57	81	94	42	30	86
	47	30	66	72	30								
10X19	80	88	58	36	30	89	38	78	87	93	30	95	30
	49	30	35	76	97	41							
10X20	90	67	37	44	30	30	89	30	58	97	91	96	65
	72	30	63	66	91	30	30						
10X21	30	63	56	30	66	91	78	50	82	30	50	79	88
	41	33	30	99	96	30	88	87					
10X22	60	78	49	30	30	39	82	30	50	83	61	62	51
	30	32	30	98	30	30	83	61	31				
10X23	82	30	83	35	46	30	74	30	30	30	92	32	30
	44	51	80	37	53	86	30	60	69	30			
10X24	30	30	30	30	88	30	30	66	80	30	30	99	30
	30	37	30	82	62	30	30	30	30	64	79		
10X25	30	30	74	30	40	47	30	30	35	50	59	89	74
	60	76	30	37	90	43	68	89	30	93	32	77	

APPENDIX 2 DATA ON PROCESSING TIMES OF JOBS IN REPLICATION 2

This appendix gives the processing times for the jobs on machine 1 in replication 2 for the numbers 2, 3, 4, 5, 6, 7, 8, 9, and 10, correspondingly, from Table A.2.1 to Table A.2.9. There are 11 to 25 jobs in each table.

Let,

n be the number of jobs

m be the number of machines

s_i be the speed of the machine i, where i = 1, 2,3, ..., m.

t_{1j} be the processing time of the job j on the machine 1, where j = 1, 2, 3, ..., n.

The following formula provides the processing times of a given job j on the machines ranging from 2 to m.

$t_{ij} = t_{1j}/s_i$, where i ranges from 2 to m.

Therefore, the above equation may be used to calculate the processing time of a job on the other machines if the processing time of the job on machine 1 is known. For each job, the processing time on machine 1 alone is provided in this appendix. The programme itself will use the above formula to calculate each job's processing time on the other machine.

Table A.2.1 Processing Times of Jobs on Machine 1 When the Number of Machines is 2

Problem Size	Job Number												
	1	2	3	4	5	6	7	8	9	10	11	12	13
	14	15	16	17	18	19	20	21	22	23	24	25	
2X11	74	33	30	30	30	84	93	30	30	49	44		
2X12	33	91	30	34	30	30	71	35	38	91	30	66	
2X13	51	57	30	55	77	30	95	30	39	30	55	30	30
2X14	37	86	48	55	95	62	93	30	30	30	79	81	30
	69												
2X15	38	46	30	78	61	47	30	57	63	51	30	30	67
	88	77											
2X16	30	30	30	30	30	53	86	70	34	92	85	52	79
	30	30	92										
2X17	60	84	48	90	33	94	55	82	42	34	60	30	90
	30	30	71	35									
2X18	30	30	42	30	84	62	36	55	67	43	30	30	89
	30	51	35	30	60								
2X19	57	30	43	40	33	72	96	30	98	82	81	48	96
	74	69	30	30	30	30							
2X20	47	98	30	48	30	96	96	30	37	93	86	30	97
	73	93	86	68	81	36	78						
2X21	48	30	30	30	90	56	33	72	58	38	53	39	30
	57	30	63	30	30	40	47	30					
2X22	30	30	66	75	92	78	30	30	30	30	30	57	81
	53	99	95	53	30	68	50	30	88				
2X23	30	30	30	30	39	32	46	94	77	63	40	75	68
	30	66	30	67	30	79	34	30	64	93			
2X24	30	30	30	93	76	83	30	50	51	39	30	84	44
	30	30	31	99	78	30	50	94	55	30	49		
2X25	66	60	64	35	48	30	85	90	49	46	54	76	41
	48	42	58	84	77	30	57	71	88	77	30	96	

Table A.2.2 Processing Times of Jobs on Machine 1 When the Number of Machines is 3

Problem Size	Job Number												
	1	2	3	4	5	6	7	8	9	10	11	12	13
	14	15	16	17	18	19	20	21	22	23	24	25	
3X11	30	32	57	51	53	30	94	48	61	30	30		
3X12	60	61	35	30	94	63	39	30	88	88	73	30	
3X13	30	30	30	40	90	30	30	88	30	30	96	62	36
3X14	93	30	54	30	46	45	78	60	62	30	49	93	47
	49												
3X15	88	30	33	30	41	30	30	45	38	93	30	70	66
	30	92											
3X16	69	70	40	30	30	82	94	94	30	71	39	51	84
	30	84	76										
3X17	50	30	93	30	85	30	30	75	38	52	71	30	36
	30	43	60	30									
3X18	83	53	30	75	32	39	83	72	82	87	57	30	84
	30	30	30	30	33								
3X19	50	97	30	30	64	66	87	30	65	36	86	30	90
	99	30	67	36	76	55							
3X20	85	91	30	30	96	30	38	30	30	81	85	66	30
	78	66	33	30	61	95	44						
3X21	30	60	85	35	79	61	88	37	71	30	44	30	74
	96	70	73	56	30	68	30	30					
3X22	**30**	**51**	**80**	**38**	**30**	**30**	**68**	**30**	**44**	**90**	30	55	42
	30	**30**	**80**	**50**	**47**	**84**	**56**	**83**	**92**				
3X23	38	47	77	35	59	57	52	30	96	97	30	70	61
	85	30	43	60	61	91	30	41	35	38			
3X24	95	74	57	35	42	49	30	56	38	30	43	30	65
	76	90	30	30	81	65	30	30	30	50	77		
3X25	80	62	30	81	40	87	43	78	86	72	51	94	38
	34	33	67	96	55	30	76	30	30	45	30	57	

Table A.2.3 Processing Times of Jobs on Machine 1 When the Number of Machines is 4

Probl em Size	Job Number												
	1	**2**	**3**	**4**	**5**	**6**	**7**	**8**	**9**	**10**	**11**	**12**	**13**
	14	**15**	**16**	**17**	**18**	**19**	**20**	**21**	**22**	**23**	**24**	**25**	
4X11	30	71	67	30	33	30	42	38	30	93	92		
4X12	30	69	69	88	89	58	30	30	30	44	30	43	
4X13	83	48	70	51	81	30	30	30	72	92	53	98	30
4X14	31	93	37	33	30	52	30	43	89	30	98	30	87
	52												
4X15	50	97	81	30	30	30	33	81	30	98	43	87	30
	72	30											
4X16	55	98	87	30	53	89	79	61	30	87	54	51	38
	35	94	30										
4X17	41	30	91	48	73	30	30	64	79	43	43	30	55
	63	74	79	30									
4X18	46	55	65	93	30	92	36	58	30	30	59	62	30
	30	84	30	41	49								
4X19	48	49	47	70	95	30	30	80	33	30	81	92	30
	75	30	69	30	30	80							
4X20	89	86	87	30	30	30	66	30	34	59	96	45	37
	85	41	67	30	78	97	30						
4X21	76	30	36	96	42	67	75	99	96	40	74	74	84
	66	53	89	30	30	41	90	31					
4X22	88	44	93	30	61	39	93	89	67	98	30	96	30
	31	37	40	30	56	60	30	62	96				
4X23	38	94	30	98	64	51	82	78	30	34	30	93	61
	63	80	33	53	74	30	47	81	30	99			
4X24	83	33	30	79	59	81	50	78	61	30	33	30	63
	30	30	30	68	30	59	30	84	30	33	45		
4X25	30	76	97	74	86	30	70	35	82	30	43	41	30
	41	30	92	59	91	30	30	87	94	72	80	30	

Table A.2.4 Processing Times of Jobs on Machine 1 When the Number of Machines is 5

Problem Size	Job Number												
	1	2	3	4	5	6	7	8	9	10	11	12	13
	14	15	16	17	18	19	20	21	22	23	24	25	
5X11	30	30	36	57	76	95	59	76	89	73	99		
5X12	56	77	56	34	30	97	79	43	91	30	40	30	
5X13	80	35	64	36	30	30	81	30	66	30	34	30	54
5X14	78	30	30	30	30	30	41	96	55	30	98	87	30
	30												
5X15	39	30	90	30	30	30	62	87	58	77	30	30	33
	57	86											
5X16	30	30	30	30	57	45	94	99	48	55	47	30	53
	30	74	30										
5X17	96	82	97	34	92	49	55	30	30	30	30	30	30
	30	62	34	81									
5X18	90	79	62	89	30	33	53	77	93	50	62	95	34
	70	30	30	30	30								
5X19	30	43	84	90	76	30	97	93	65	84	66	72	90
	47	91	88	30	75	66							
5X20	30	30	30	30	46	47	30	30	68	30	81	30	30
	55	31	32	30	30	72	30						
5X21	30	54	64	96	79	84	30	71	83	30	81	71	30
	98	30	54	75	57	96	68	56					
5X22	68	30	30	91	87	30	96	30	59	59	52	62	56
	30	30	73	41	38	85	30	59	73				
5X23	44	55	45	30	84	78	71	85	30	30	30	57	86
	30	30	81	79	74	30	30	44	42	51			
5X24	34	97	44	92	95	84	93	36	30	88	30	80	30
	51	95	67	55	30	71	52	93	61	53	86		
5X25	75	84	97	35	30	49	30	30	56	74	83	64	30
	30	88	30	77	30	49	30	77	30	68	30	71	

Table A.2.5 Processing Times of Jobs on Machine 1 When the Number of Machines is 6

Problem Size	Job Number												
	1	2	3	4	5	6	7	8	9	10	11	12	13
	14	15	16	17	18	19	20	21	22	23	24	25	
6X11	36	78	32	49	30	30	30	69	30	68	30		
6X12	30	30	97	31	57	40	80	85	30	53	32	76	
6X13	30	30	90	30	36	30	36	30	98	35	39	76	41
6X14	61	30	52	30	75	78	30	30	30	53	72	30	98
	30												
6X15	83	30	30	64	96	30	76	30	89	30	30	41	30
	30	30											
6X16	44	30	83	92	55	93	30	66	30	67	30	76	30
	30	57	51										
6X17	30	87	30	30	30	53	30	34	30	55	99	48	30
	30	49	30	84									
6X18	65	92	48	34	30	30	93	79	68	76	66	30	48
	88	30	31	30	30								
6X19	31	58	30	30	79	85	48	34	96	30	30	30	30
	51	67	84	83	30	81							
6X20	54	57	50	61	75	34	30	39	60	54	69	30	87
	62	30	89	32	30	30	98						
6X21	30	99	79	30	35	97	34	44	73	49	30	84	31
	62	30	75	38	35	52	69	38					
6X22	30	30	30	30	51	93	30	73	41	79	32	89	30
	35	82	30	95	30	30	75	30	75				
6X23	98	30	30	88	37	81	30	48	30	90	75	71	30
	96	52	78	30	90	64	87	79	40	85			
6X24	31	43	78	30	30	39	30	88	59	30	32	30	36
	75	30	46	53	60	79	50	30	70	73	30		
6X25	96	30	49	86	30	66	95	74	30	88	30	30	87
	30	84	67	95	70	87	57	57	30	69	63	30	

Table A.2.6 Processing Times of Jobs on Machine 1 When the Number of Machines is 7

Problem Size	Job Number												
	1	2	3	4	5	6	7	8	9	10	11	12	13
	14	15	16	17	18	19	20	21	22	23	24	25	
7X11	77	72	39	46	96	53	98	87	45	30	30		
7X12	77	30	68	31	30	96	30	55	42	74	30	90	
7X13	30	84	32	58	43	93	45	30	57	45	34	45	49
7X14	30	51	50	91	48	56	39	41	74	76	30	61	46
	90												
7X15	30	66	52	34	30	89	30	33	30	83	30	64	82
	35	44											
7X16	32	71	30	85	83	30	50	30	35	77	30	52	35
	62	30	30										
7X17	42	83	50	75	38	80	30	60	56	34	69	55	41
	92	87	51	30									
7X18	30	40	30	64	79	30	30	30	30	60	82	59	42
	30	79	30	82	86								
7X19	70	50	53	82	77	67	30	90	98	91	30	51	44
	94	95	30	30	30	61							
7X20	93	43	72	89	96	94	65	30	30	30	30	30	62
	66	85	83	92	52	30	62						
7X21	38	86	31	76	68	30	90	30	30	30	38	30	58
	64	61	71	30	30	67	97	30					
5022	30	62	67	71	90	58	30	98	62	30	78	30	47
	76	57	80	30	84	37	50	88	61				
7X23	30	41	58	52	73	74	73	83	78	93	39	41	59
	30	72	86	30	41	86	78	67	77	30			
7X24	41	30	30	30	41	30	30	30	96	30	80	30	30
	99	98	97	30	99	72	75	30	89	47	39		
7X25	83	41	62	30	94	31	48	30	42	63	48	42	30
	30	63	53	59	51	30	84	30	52	65	30	30	

Table A.2.7 Processing Times of Jobs on Machine 1 When the Number of Machines is 8

Problem Size	Job Number												
	1	2	3	4	5	6	7	8	9	10	11	12	13
	14	15	16	17	18	19	20	21	22	23	24	25	
8X11	30	97	98	53	59	69	30	65	30	30	87		
8X12	30	74	30	52	95	93	86	39	30	75	30	30	
8X13	65	79	94	71	89	35	67	55	62	73	30	87	30
8X14	72	39	40	49	36	30	30	38	99	50	88	30	47
	81												
8X15	90	46	74	72	30	30	56	50	45	42	52	94	44
	84	33											
8X16	47	30	75	32	68	30	49	30	99	80	97	30	60
	38	30	76										
8X17	73	75	30	30	30	30	69	34	30	85	30	30	36
	30	98	45	53									
8X18	76	90	41	72	30	81	31	37	44	68	30	32	30
	30	34	30	70	68								
8X19	30	30	36	99	67	62	67	30	98	85	85	30	63
	67	31	30	30	43	33							
8X20	61	30	57	90	30	94	55	92	38	75	30	55	82
	71	66	86	34	30	30	72						
8X21	39	33	30	93	60	39	30	65	58	30	70	30	30
	52	97	97	30	77	30	53	85					
8X22	51	39	30	30	81	81	30	90	30	79	75	30	30
	64	63	40	30	82	56	43	30	46				
8X23	50	30	67	30	42	30	57	30	40	77	30	30	30
	42	52	39	30	83	30	41	56	60	44			
8X24	75	30	73	81	64	81	48	39	60	30	46	30	30
	30	90	38	41	82	30	30	30	30	30	87		
8X25	31	56	30	30	30	93	74	30	55	30	75	52	30
	30	40	45	30	30	73	73	55	60	30	30	77	

Table A.2.8 Processing Times of Jobs on Machine 1 When the Number of Machines is 9

Problem Size	Job Number												
	1	2	3	4	5	6	7	8	9	10	11	12	13
	14	15	16	17	18	19	20	21	22	23	24	25	
9X11	30	60	30	43	52	30	88	47	46	43	30		
9X12	74	64	30	64	94	30	61	95	82	49	84	30	
9X13	64	72	30	70	88	90	31	30	30	42	82	69	53
9X14	56	99	60	78	30	41	93	30	47	37	60	84	32
	48												
9X15	62	99	47	46	63	37	31	30	67	46	71	30	30
	54	30											
9X16	30	30	86	30	32	30	30	95	38	97	30	30	30
	30	30	36										
9X17	51	30	30	92	91	83	30	30	76	30	69	81	59
	30	76	57	66									
9X18	30	82	30	81	30	47	30	51	82	30	62	30	39
	75	72	85	81	50								
9X19	63	85	81	75	45	30	73	98	98	94	59	74	94
	59	31	81	30	30	30							
9X20	66	92	94	99	30	50	30	30	59	66	66	40	67
	37	94	60	30	56	30	90						
9X21	73	30	98	30	40	54	30	30	30	34	90	30	63
	65	83	30	94	62	44	89	54					
9X22	49	30	36	97	93	84	30	41	73	34	30	36	68
	37	81	63	66	30	86	53	30	82				
9X23	77	30	59	34	45	78	77	99	30	53	46	33	30
	83	30	30	73	30	30	72	30	30	76			
9X24	75	78	35	57	31	36	30	35	52	35	51	30	63
	79	30	73	36	34	46	88	49	50	65	62		
9X25	65	30	60	43	46	30	85	30	79	30	47	56	38
	30	30	86	67	84	30	30	85	59	31	30	30	

Table A.2.9 Processing Times of Jobs on Machine 1 When the Number of Machines is 10

Problem Size	Job Number												
	1	2	3	4	5	6	7	8	9	10	11	12	13
	14	15	16	17	18	19	20	21	22	23	24	25	
10X11	30	30	30	75	75	83	31	89	47	41	50		
10X12	70	30	53	30	30	62	87	91	62	49	52	43	
10X13	91	30	36	50	30	38	81	30	30	30	75	30	30
10X14	49	77	94	56	78	57	77	62	30	70	32	45	55
	49												
10X15	89	30	30	30	82	92	71	79	30	71	69	30	30
	30	62											
10X16	93	56	30	30	90	30	31	30	30	52	35	30	78
	88	38	85										
10X17	30	80	30	66	87	83	33	30	43	31	67	30	31
	30	30	30	67									
10X18	53	66	58	61	30	80	41	58	30	30	30	30	77
	60	57	94	91	95								
10X19	46	77	30	81	63	30	42	30	97	30	98	61	56
	88	35	87	99	30	30							
10X20	69	80	30	56	91	35	30	76	75	73	60	51	45
	30	37	81	30	30	97	72						
10X21	40	30	86	30	73	96	47	30	95	30	39	50	63
	30	87	42	30	77	48	64	50					
10X22	37	30	87	90	30	30	34	61	85	68	47	49	70
	92	68	30	34	33	64	30	30	30				
10X23	56	30	89	39	88	63	30	30	30	49	51	31	30
	47	30	30	61	30	66	30	96	61	55			
10X24	71	30	88	75	39	67	37	30	38	30	30	65	69
	30	82	87	91	30	39	30	30	30	30	49		
10X25	35	40	56	63	52	47	91	30	64	62	30	30	54
	68	30	30	30	33	34	59	69	73	77	61	94	

REFERENCE

1. Agarwal, A., Colak, S., Jacob, V.S. and Pirkul, H., 2006, Heuristics and augmented neural networks for task scheduling with non-identical machines, European Jouranl of Operational Research, Vol.175, No.1, pp.296-317.
2. Alain Guinet, 1995, Scheduling independent jobs on uniform parallel machines to minimize tardiness criteria, Journal of Intelligent Manufacturing, Vol.6, No.2, pp.95-103.
3. Albers, S., Fiat, A. and Woeginger, G., 2002, Online algorithms, Dagstuhl Seminar.
4. Angelelli, E., Speranza, M.G. and Tuza, Z., Semi-online scheduling on two uniform processors, Theoretical Computer Science, DOI:10.1016/j.tcs.2007.12.005, Article in Press.
5. Azar, Y. and Epstein, L., 1997, On-line machine covering, Proceedings of 5th ESA conference, pp.23-36.
6. Azar, Y. and Epstein, L., 1998a, On-line machine covering, Journal of Scheduling, Vol.1, No.2, pp.67-77.
7. Azar, Y. and Epstein, L., 1998b, Approximation schemes for covering and scheduling on related machines, Proceedings of the 1st Workshop on Approximation Algorithms for Combinatorial Optimization Problems (APPROX '98), Also, in Lecture Notes in Comput.Sci. 1444, pp.39-47, Springer-Verlag, 1998.
8. Bahram Alidaee and Ahmad Ahmadian, 1993, Two parallel machine sequencing problems involving controllable job processing times, European Journal of Operational Research, Vol.70, No.3, pp.335-341.
9. Bahram Alidaee and Ahmad Ahmadian, 1996, Scheduling on a single processor with variable speed, Information Processing Letters, Vol.60, No.4, pp.189-193.
10. Balakrishnan, N., Kanet, J.J. and Sridharan, S., 1999, Early/tardy scheduling with sequence dependent setups on uniform parallel machines, Computers & Operations Research, Vol.26, No.2, pp.127-141.
11. Baruah, S. and Goossens, J., 2003, Rate-monotonic scheduling on uniform multiprocessors, IEEE Trans. Computers, Vol.57, No.7, pp.966-970.
12. Baruah, S., 2001, Scheduling periodic tasks on uniform multiprocessors, Information Processing Letters, Vol.80, No.2, pp.97-104.
13. Bekki, O.B. and Meral Azizoglu, (2007, In Press), Operational fixed interval scheduling problem on uniform parallel machines, International Journal of Production Economics, DOI:10.1016/j.ijpe.2007.06.004.
14. Berit Johannes, 2006, Scheduling parallel jobs to minimize the makespan, Journal of Scheduling, Vol.9, pp.433-452.

15. Bilge, U., Kirac, F., Kurtulan, M. and Pekgun, P, 2004, A tabu search algorithm for parallel machine total tardiness problem, Computers and Operations Research, Vol. 31, No.3, pp.397-414.

16. Blazewicz, J., 1984, Minimizing mean weighted information loss with preemptable tasks and parallel processors, Technology and Science of Informatics, Vol.3, pp.415-420.

17. Blazewicz, J. and Bouvry, P., Guinand, F. and Trystram, D., 1996, Scheduling complete intrees on two uniform processors with communication delays, Information Processing Letters, Vol.58, No.5, pp.255-263.

18. Blazewicz, J. and Finke, G., 1987, Minimizing mean weighted execution time loss on identical and uniform processors, Information processing Letters, Vol.24, No.4, pp.259-263.

19. Bulfin, R.L. and Parker, R.G., 1980, Scheduling jobs on two facilities to minimize makespan, Management Science, Vol.26, No.2, pp. 202-214.

20. Burkard, R.E. and He, Y., 1998, A note on MULTIFIT scheduling for uniform machines, Computing, Vol.61, No.3, pp.277-283.

21. Burkard, R.E., He, Y. and Kellerer, H., 1998, A linear compound algorithm for uniform machine scheduling, Computing, Col.61, No.1, pp.1-9.

22. Chandra Chekuri and Michael Bender, 1999, An efficient approximation algorithm for minimizing makespan on uniformly related machines, Proceedings of IPCO'99, LNCS, pp.383-393.

23. Chandra Chekuri and Michael Bender, 2001, An efficient approximation algorithm for minimizing makespan on uniformly related machines, Journal of Algorithms, Vol.41, No.2, 212-224.

24. Chen, B., 1991, Parametric bounds for LPT scheduling on uniform processors, Acta Mathematicae Applicateae, Sinica, Vol.7, pp.67-73.

25. Chen, B., 1991, Tighter bounds for MULTIFIT scheduling on uniform processors, Discrete Applied mathematics, Vol. 31, pp.227-260.

26. Cheng, T.C.E., Ng, C.T. and Viadimir Kotov, 2006, A new algorithm for online uniform-machine scheduling to minimize the makespan, Information Processing Letters, Vol.99, No.3, pp.102-105.

27. Chhajed, D., 1988, A note on minimizing the maximum deviation of job completion time about a common due-date, Applied Mathematics Letters, Vol.1, No.2, pp.161-163.

28. Chien-Hung Lin and Ching-Jong Liao, 2007, Makespan minimization for multiple uniform machines, Computers & Industrial Engineering, Doi:10.1016/j.cie.2007.11.009

29. Ching Jong Liao and Chien-Hung Lin, 2003, Makespan minimization for two uniform parallel machines, International Journal of Production Economics, Vol.84, No.2, pp.205-213.

30. Christos Koulamas and George J. Kyparisis, 2000, Scheduling on uniform parallel machines to minimize maximum lateness, Operations Research Letters, Vol.26, pp.175-179.

31. Christos Koulamas and George J. Kyparisis, 2004, Makespan minimization on uniform parallel machines with release times, European Journal of Operational Research, Vol.157, pp. 262-266.

32. Chudak, F.A. and Shmoys, D.B., 1997, An efficient approximation algorithm for minimizing makespan on uniformly related machines, Proceedings of the Eighth Annual ACM-SIAM Symposium on Discrete Algorithms, pp.581-590.

33. Chudak, F.A. and Shmoys, D.B., 1999, Approximation algorithm for precedence-constrained scheduling problems on parallel machines that run at different speeds, Journal of Algorithms, Vol.20, No.2, pp.323-343.

34. Coffman Jr., E.G. and Graham, R.L., 1972, Optimal scheduling for two-processor systems, Acta Informatica, Vol.1, No.3, pp.200-213.

35. Dessouky, M.I. and Marcellus, R.L., 1998, Scheduling identical jobs on uniform parallel machines with random processing times, Computers and Industrial Engineering, Vol.35, Nos.1-2, pp.109-112.

36. Dessouky, M.M., 1998, Scheduling identical jobs with unequal ready times on uniform parallel machines to minimize the maximum lateness, Computers & Industrial Engineering, Vol.34, No.4, pp.793-806.

37. Donglei Du, 2004, Optimal preemptive semi-online scheduling on two uniform processors, Information Processing letters, Vol.92, No.5, pp.219-223.

38. Drozdowski, M., Blazewicz, J, Formanowicz, P., Kubiak, W. and Schmidt, G., 2000, Scheduling preemptable tasks on uniform processors with limited availability for maximum lateness criterion, VII International Workshop on Project Management Scheduling, pp.118-120.

39. Epstein, L. and Sgall, J., 2000, A lower bound for on-line scheduling on uniformly related machines, Operations Research Letters, Vol.26, No.1, pp.17-22.

40. Epstein, L. and Favrholdt, L.M., 2002 Optimal non-preemptive semi-online scheduling on two related machines, Proceedings of the 27th Symposium on Mathematical Foundations of Computer Science, Volume 2420 of Lecture Notes in Computer Science, pp.245-256, Springer, 2002.

41. Epstein, L. and Favrholdt, L.M., 2002, Optimal preemptive semi-online scheduling to minimize makespan on two related machines, Operations Research Letters, Vol.30, No.4, pp.269-275.

42. Epstein, L. and Favrholdt, L.M., 2005, Optimal non-preemptive semi-online scheduling on two related machines, Journal of Algorithms, Vol.57, No.1, pp.49-73.

43. Epstein, L. and Sgall, J., 1999, Approximation schemes for scheduling on uniformly related and identical parallel machines, Proceedings of 7th Annual European Symposium on Algorithms, pp.151-162.

44. Epstein, L. and Sgall, J., 2004, Approximation schemes for scheduling on uniformly related and identical parallel machines, Algorithmica, Vol.39, No.1, pp.43-57.

45. Epstein, L., 2001(a), Optimal preemptive on-line scheduling on uniform processors with non-decreasing speed ratios, Operations Research Letters, Vol.29, No.2, pp.93-98.

46. Epstein, L., 2001(b), Optimal preemptive scheduling on uniform processors with non-decreasing speed ratios, Proceedings of 18th STACS, pp.230-237.

47. Epstein, L., Noga, J., Seiden, S.S., Sgall, J. and Woeginger, G.J., 2001, Randomized on-line scheduling on two uniform machines, Journal of Scheduling, Vol.4, No.2, pp.71-92.

48. Epstein, L., Noga, J., Seiden, S.S., Sgall, J. and Woeginger, G.J., 1999, Randomized on-line scheduling on two uniform machines, Proceedings of the Tenth Annual ACM-SIAM Symposium on Discrete Algorithms, pp.317-326.

49. Federgruen, A. and Groenevelt, H., 1986, Preemptive scheduling of uniform machines by ordinary network flow techniques, Management Science, Vol.32, No.3, pp.341-349.

50. Friesen, D.K. and Langston, M.A., 1983, Bounds for multifit scheduling on uniform processors, SIAM Journal on Computing, Vol.12, pp.60-70.

51. Friesen, D.K., 1987, Tighter bounds for LPT scheduling on uniform processors, SIAM Journal on Computing, Vol.16, No.3, pp.554-560.

52. Funk, S., Goossens, J. and Baruah, S., 2001, Online scheduling on uniform multiprocessors, Proceedings of the IEEE Real-Time Systems Symposium, pp.183-192.

53. Gonzalez, T. and Sahni, S., 1978, Preemptive scheduling of uniform processor systems, Journal of Association of Comput. Mach., Vol.25, pp.92-101.

54. Gonzalez, T., Ibarra, O.H., and Sahni, S., 1977, Bounds for LPT schedules, on uniform processors, SIAM Journal on Computing, No.6, pp.155-166.

55. Gonzalez, T.F., Joseph, Y.T.L. and Pinedo, M., 2006, Minimizing total completion time on uniform machines with deadline constraints, ACM Transactions on Algorithms, Vol.2, No.1 pp.95-115.

56. Graham, R.L., 1969, Bounds for multiprocessing timing anomalies, SIAM Journal of Applied Mathematics, Vol.17, No.2, pp.416-429.

57. Gregory Dobson, 1984, Scheduling independent tasks on uniform processors, SIAM Journal of Computing, Vol.13, No.4, pp.705-716.

58. Gregory Dobson, 1984, Scheduling independent tasks on uniform processors, SIAM Journal on Computing, Vol.13, No.4, pp.705-716.

59. Gur Mosheiov and Assaf Sarig, 2007, Due-date assignment on uniform machines, European Journal of Operational Research, (Article in Press).

60. He, Y. and Jiang, Y., 2005, Optimal semi-online preemptive algorithms for machine covering on two uniform machines, Theoretical Computer Science, Vol.339, No.2-3, pp.293-314.

61. He, Y. and Min, X., 2000, On-line uniform machine scheduling with rejection, Computing, Vol.65, No.1, pp.1-12.

62. Hochbaum, D.S and Shmoys, D.B., 1988, A polynomial approximation scheme for scheduling on uniform processors: Using the dual approximation approach, SIAM J.Compt. Vol.17, No.3, pp.539-551.

63. Horowiz, E. and Sahni, S., 1976, Exact and approximate algorithms for scheduling nonidentical processors, Journal of the ACM, Vol.23, No.2, pp.317-327.

64. Ibarra, O,H. and Kim, C.E., 1977, Heuristic algorithms for scheduling independent tasks on nonidentical processors, Journal of the ACM, Vol.24, No.2, pp.280-289.

65. Ishi, H., Martel, C., Masuda, T. and Nishida, T., 1985, A generalized uniform processor system, Operations Research, Vol.33, No.2, pp.346-362.

66. Jaffe, J., 1980, Efficient scheduling of tasks without full use of processor resources, Theoretical Computer Science, Vol.26, pp.22-35.

67. Kis, T. and Kapolnai, R., 2007, Approximation and auctions for scheduling batches on related machines, Operations Research Letters, Vol.35, No.1, pp.61-68.

68. Kontogiannis, S., 2002, Multiple-choice assignments on uniformly related machines, ALCOM-FT Technical Report Series, 02-39.

69. Kovacs, A., 2005, Fast monotone 3-approximation algorithm for scheduling related machines, Proceedings of ESA (Also, in Lecture Notes in Computer Science, Vol.3669, pp.616-627).

70. Kovalyov, M.Y. and Shafransky, Y.M., 1998, Uniform machine scheduling of unit-time jobs subject to resource constraints, Discrete Applied Mathematics, Vol.84, No.1-3, pp.253-257.

71. Kubiak, B., Penz, B. and Trystram, D., 2002, Scheduling chains on uniform processors with communication delays, Journal of Scheduling, Vol.5, No.6, pp.459-476.

72. Kun-si Lin, 1981, Scheduling with parallel machines to minimize total job tardiness, Engineering Costs and production Economics, Vol.5, No.3-4, pp.289-296.

73. Lawler, E.L. and Martel, C.U., 1989, Preemptive scheduling of two uniform machines to minimize the number of late jobs, Operations Research, Vol.37, No.2, pp.314-318.

74. Leung, J.Y.T., Haibing Li, Michael Pinedo and Jiawei Zhang, 2007, Minimizing total weighted completion time when scheduling orders in a

flexible environment with uniform machines, Information Processing Letters, Vol. 103, No.3, pp.119-129.

75. Li, R. and Shi, L., 1998, An on-line algorithm for some uniform processor scheduling, SIAM Journal of Comput., Vol.27, No.2, pp.414-422.

76. Martel, C.U., 1988, A parallel algorithm for preemptive scheduling of uniform machines, Journal of Parallel and Distributed Computing, Vol.5, No.6, pp.700-715.

77. McCormic, S.T., and Pinedo, M., 1995, Scheduling n independent jobs on m uniform machines with both flow time and makespan objectives: A parametric analysis, ORSA Journal of Computing, Vol.7, pp.63-77.

78. Meral Azizoglu and Omer Kirca, 1998, Tardiness minimization on parallel machines, International Journal of Production Economics, Vol.55, No.2, pp.163-168.

79. Meral Azizoglu and Omer Kirca, 1999, On the minimization of total weighted flow time with identical and uniform parallel machines, European Journal of Operational Research, Vol.113, pp.91-100.

80. Mireault, P., Orlin, J.B., and Vohra, R.V., 1997, A parametric worst case analysis of the LPT heuristic for two uniform machines, Operations Research, Vol.45, No.1, pp.116-125.

81. Naofumi, I., Shunji, T. and Mitsuhiko, A., 2003, Minimizing total tardiness on uniform parallel machines under human resource constraint, Proceedings of the Annual Conference of the Institute of Systems, Control and Information Engineers, Vol.47th, No.419-420.

82. Pandelis, D.G., 2007, Optimal preemptive scheduling on uniform machines with discounted flow time objectives, European Journal of Operational Research, Vol.177, No.1, pp.630-637.

83. Panneerselvam, R and Kanagalingam, S, 1998, Modelling parallel processors with different processing speeds of single machine scheduling problem to minimize makespan, Industrial Engineering Journal, Vol. XVII, No.6, pp.16-19.

84. Panneerselvam, R and Kanagalingam, S, 1999, Simple heuristic for single machine scheduling problem with two parallel processors having varying speeds to minimize makespan, Industrial Engineering Journal, Vol. XVIII, No.6, pp.2-8.

85. Panneerselvam, R, 2005, Production and Operations Management (Second Edition), Prentice-Hall of India, New Delhi.

86. Prabuddha De and Thomas E.Morton, 1980, Scheduling to minimize makespan on unequal parallel processors, Decision Sciences, Vol.11, pp.586-602.

87. Ruize-Torres, A.J., Lopez, F.J. and Ho, J.C., 2007, Scheduling uniform parallel machines subject to a secondary resource to minimize the number of tardy jobs, European Journal of Operational Research, Vol. 179, No.2, pp.302-315.

88. Sahni, S. and Cho, Y., 1980, Scheduling independent tasks with due times on a uniform processor system, Journal of the ACM, Vol.27, No.3, pp.550-563.

89. Senthilkumar, P., Development of Metaheuristics to Minimize Makespan in Single Machine Scheduling Problem with Uniform Parallel Machines and Their Comparisons, Ph.D. Thesis, Anna University, 2012.

90. Shachnai, H., Tamir, T. and Woeginger, G.J., 2002, Minimizing makespan and preemption costs on a system of uniform machines, Proceedings of the 10th European Symposium on Algorithms, pp.859-871.

91. Shakhlevich, N.V. and Strusevich, V.A., 2007, Preemptive scheduling on uniform parallel machines with controllable job processing times, Algorithmica, DOI 10.1007/s00453-007-9091-9, (Online).

92. Tan, Z. and He, Y. and Epstein, L., 2005, Optimal on-line algorithms for the uniform machine scheduling problem with ordinal data, Information and Computation, Vol.196, No.1, pp.57-70.

93. Tan, Z. and He, Y., 2001, Semi-on-line scheduling with ordinal data on two uniform machines, Operations Research Letters, Vol.28, No.5, pp.221-231.

94. Tuong, N.H., Soukhal, A. and Jean-Charles Billaut, 2007, Uniform parallel machine scheduling problem with a common due date to minimize total weighted tardiness, MAPSP Conference.

95. Vahid, S, Mohmoud, N. and Mohsen, K., 2007, Deadline scheduling with processor affinity and feasibility check on uniform machines, Computer and Information Technology, Vol.16-19, pp.793-798.

96. Vestjens, A, 1998, Scheduling uniform machines on-line requires nondecreasing speed ratios, Mathematical Programming, Vol.82, No.2, pp.225-234.

97. Viniclus Amaral Armentano and Moacir Fellzardo de Franca Filho, 2007, Minimizing total tardiness in parallel machine scheduling with setup times: An adaptive momory-based GRASP approach, European Journal of Operations Research, Vol.183, No.1, pp.100-114.

98. Wein, J and Williamson, D.P., 1990, On-line scheduling of parallel machines, Technical Report, Massachusetts, Inst of Tech, Cambridge Lab for Computer Science, p.18.

99. Wen, J. and Du, D., 1998, Preemptive on-line scheduling for two uniform processors, Operations Research Letters, Vol.23, pp.113-116.

100. Woeginger, G.J., 2000, A comment on scheduling on uniform machines under chain-type precedence constraints, Operations Research Letters, Vol.26, No.3, pp.107-109.

101. Zhi-Long Chen and Warren B.Powell, 1999, Solving parallel machine scheduling problems by column generation, INFORMS Journal on Computing, Vol.11, pp.78-94.

INDEX

ABOUT THE AUTHOR

P. Senthilkumar, PhD, is Deputy general Manager, Platform Program Management – mStar Platform, Farm Division at Mahindra and Mahindra Limited, Mahindra Research Valley, Chengalpattu, Tamil Nadu. He has about 18 years + of industry experience in process planning and programme management. Previously, he has served at Valeo Minda Electrical Systems India Pvt. Ltd, Ashok Leyland, Foton Motors, and Lucas TVS Ltd. Dr Senthilkumar has published several research papers in leading national and international journals and has authored several textbooks. His areas of research interest include Project management, New Product Development, Simulation, Production scheduling, Automated Guided Vehicle Systems (AGVS) scheduling, etc.